FAST BREADS

BISCUITS

↗ STROMBOLI

LOAF

POPOVERS

ROLLS

ROLLS

BRIOCHE

TWISTS

CRESCENTS

SCONES

↘ STRATA

MUFFINS

TOAST
ROUND

WAFFLES

FAST
BREADS

ROLLS

GOUGERES

50 RECIPES FOR EASY, DELICIOUS BREAD

BY ELINOR KLIVANS
PHOTOGRAPHS BY
SUSIE CUSHNER

RYE

YEAST

TWIST

DOUGH

MUFFINS
DOUGHNUTS
BUNS

CRUMPETS

CHRONICLE BOOKS
SAN FRANCISCO

DEDICATION

*For the four generations of my bread-baking and
bread-loving family and for Jeff, who baked real good bread*

Library of Congress
Cataloging-in-Publication
Data available.

ISBN 978-0-8118-6570-8

Manufactured in China

Designed by Lesley Feldman
Prop styling by
Randi Brookman Harris
Food styling by Carrie Purcell

10 9 8 7 6 5 4 3 2 1

Chronicle Books LLC
680 Second Street
San Francisco, California 94107
www.chroniclebooks.com

ACKNOWLEDGMENTS

 It takes a village to make a book happen: an agent, a publishing team, a photographer, a food stylist, family, friends, testers, and lots of listeners. Thank you all.

My agent, Judith Weber; editorial director Bill LeBlond; editor Sarah Billingsley; copyeditor Sharon Silva; photographer Susie Cushner; food stylist Carrie Purcell; Doug Ogan, Anne Donnard, Ben Hasman, Peter Perez, David Hawk, and the fabulous team at Chronicle Books.

My family, who care, support, and encourage me; make me laugh; and are baking partners: my dad, Laura, Michael, Charlie, and Oliver; Kate, Peter, Madison, Max, Sadie, and Kip.

My supporters and friends, who ate a lot of bread and gave a lot of encouragement: Flo Braker, Sue Chase, Michael Drons, Susan Dunning, Maureen Egan, Carole and Woody Emanuel, Rosalee and Chris Glass, Karen and Michael Good, Kat and Howard Grossman, Faith and David Hague, Helen and Reg Hall, Carolyn and Ted Hoffman, Alice and Norman Klivans, Susan Lasky, Robert Laurence, Rosie Levitan, Gordon Paine, Joan and Graham Phaup, Janet and Alan Roberts, Pam and Stephen Ross, Louise and Erv Shames, Barbara and Max Steinheimer, Kathy Stiefel, Carol Witham, Elaine and Wil Wolfson, and Jeffrey Young.

The brave and thorough testers: Jennifer and Howie Goldsmith (the day before Jennifer gave birth), Howard Grossman, Cheryl Matevish, Taylor Mudge, Dawn Ryan, Allyson Shames, Louise Shames, Kate Steinheimer, and Laura Williams.

CONTENTS

INTRODUCTION ↗

If I were stranded on a desert island, I know exactly what my choice for survival food would be: bread and butter. Biscuits, muffins, cinnamon buns, yeast breads—I like them all. I have been baking bread since I was a teenager, and today it is still a pleasure to turn a few simple ingredients into a colossal popover or see a buttermilk loaf rise high in the oven and then eat it.

All the breads I bake take only a short time to put together, and then I fit finishing them—usually shaping and baking them—around my schedule. I assemble scones, corn bread, crusty loaves, and doughnuts in minutes. I make yeast-leavened sticky buns, brioche, dark rye, and a crusty multigrain loaf that sit in the refrigerator for as long as several days. They wait to be baked until I have the time or the inclination, and then they rise just once in the pan. My buttery rolls, cheese loaves, buttermilk loaf, focaccia, and nut-and-fruit whole-wheat rounds are all batter breads, made from a soft yeast dough. They are mixed with an electric mixer, in a food processor, or by hand, and rise just once in the pan immediately after mixing and shaping. Morning toast and crumpets, lunchtime sandwiches, and dinner rolls—bread is an important part of every meal. Good bread is a given; the nurturing, pride, and enjoyment are your gifts.

Years ago, David Gayson, the late American essayist and journalist, aptly wrote, "Talk of joy: there may be things better than beef stew and baked potatoes and home-made bread—there may be."

BREAD BASICS

Here are the good ideas—everything from my favorite pans to tips on leaveners to how to choose the best ingredients—I have learned from a lifetime of bread baking.

EQUIPMENT

Most of the pans for making bread, including baking sheets, muffin tins, and loaf pans are probably already in your kitchen. If you do go shopping, remember to buy good quality pans and tools. You will work more efficiently and your new purchases will last for years.

Bread Pans

Heavy-gauge aluminum conducts heat evenly and does not warp or bend with repeated use, making it a good choice for bread pans of all shapes and sizes. Baking sheets with a low rim on one or more sides simplify sliding baked breads onto a wire rack to cool. Measurements suitable for home ovens range from about 15 by 12 in to about 17 by 14 in.

A jelly-roll pan is a baking sheet with a 1-in rim on all sides. The most common size is about 15 by 10 in. I use this pan when making Buttery Rowies (page 86) to prevent the excess butter from dripping onto the oven.

The loaf pan I use most often has a capacity of about 8 cups and measures about 9 by 5 by 3 in. Round, rectangular, and square pans in varying sizes should have 2-in sides. Ceramic baking dishes in these shapes are good oven-to-table choices.

You will need a tube pan with a permanently fixed bottom, and a diameter of 9½ in or 10 in. A fixed-bottom tube pan, which is especially useful for batter breads and bread puddings, is somewhat harder to find than a pan with a removable bottom, the classic angel food cake pan. The 9½-in one-piece tube can be difficult to locate, too, but Nordic Ware makes an excellent one-piece 10-in tube with a 12-cup capacity in heavy-duty aluminum. Even if your tube pan has a nonstick coating, line the bottom with parchment paper, which ensures that a large, sticky bread will release smoothly.

I use a so-called Texas muffin tin, also known as a jumbo muffin tin, for my muffin making. It has six wells, each with a capacity of 1 cup. You can use it for my Very Big Popovers (page 22), too.

Electric Mixer

A heavy-duty stand mixer with a 5-qt bowl performs any bread mixing job with ease. The mixer comes with a flat beater for beating, a wire whip for whipping, and a dough hook for kneading yeast dough. The flat beater works fine for beating batter breads and mixing and kneading soft-dough yeast breads. In the few recipes where a dough hook is preferred, I have noted it. You can use a handheld mixer with a powerful motor for any recipe that does not specify a dough hook.

Food Processor

A food processor can mix and knead bread dough in seconds, rather than minutes. If you have a standard-capacity food processor, you will need to mix most recipes in two batches, however. I find it easier to use an electric mixer or to knead by hand than to go through the process of dividing the dough. I also like the slower—but not slow— process of watching the bread dough form and the opportunity to get the "feel" of the dough as it comes together, which isn't as easy in a food processor.

Oven

The temperature inside your oven will vary about 10°F, with the upper third and the rear usually the warmest areas. If you find that your bread is burning or underbaking even though you have closely followed the temperature and timing directions in the recipes, use an oven thermometer to test your oven. Place it in the center of the oven, turn on the oven, and allow at least 20 minutes for it to preheat fully. Check the thermometer, and if it does not match the temperature on the dial, you can adjust the dial accordingly when you bake. If the temperature is too far off, have the oven checked by a professional.

I have included the position of the oven rack in each recipe, though most breads bake in the middle of the oven. Don't be tempted to bake too many items at once. Air needs to circulate around breads (or anything) as they bake, or they won't bake evenly.

INGREDIENTS

Butter, Oil & Nonstick Cooking Spray

Use unsalted butter when making breads. Its use controls the amount of salt added to a recipe because none is hidden in the butter.

When I need to add a flavorless vegetable oil to a recipe, I use corn oil or canola oil. For olive oil, I use an extra-virgin oil, made from the first pressing of the olives without the use of heat or chemicals. Taste or smell your oils often to make sure they have not turned rancid.

Nonstick cooking spray is handy for greasing pans evenly. Be sure to buy spray made from a flavorless oil.

Cornmeal

I use stone-ground cornmeal in my recipes. The corn is ground between large stones, rather than steel rollers, and is often produced by small millers. Stoneground cornmeal contains the fat-rich germ of the kernels, has a good flavor, and includes lots of appealing irregularly shaped particles. It comes in yellow, white, or blue, depending on the color of the kernels. I prefer the yellow cornmeal over the white, but it is a matter of taste and not quality and often depends on what you grew up eating. Look for stone-ground cornmeal in all colors in natural foods stores and the natural foods sections of supermarkets, and store in tightly covered containers in the refrigerator or freezer.

Eggs

For consistency, I use large eggs in my recipes. Many farm stands, farmers' markets, small shops, and even some supermarkets sell local eggs, and they are worth buying. They are fresher because they have not been transported from far away. Always store eggs in the coldest part of the refrigerator.

Flours

Wheat flour is made by grinding wheat kernels to a fine powder. I use four types of wheat flour in my recipes: unbleached all-purpose flour, unbleached bread flour, whole-wheat flour, and cake flour. I prefer unbleached all-purpose flour and bread flour because they have not been treated with chemicals to whiten them.

All-purpose flour is milled from a blend of hard and soft wheats. Bread flour is made from hard wheat and has a high protein and gluten content, which adds to the elasticity, strength, and gas-retaining properties of a dough. It is used along with other flours to make a "stronger" bread dough. The recipe for Crusty Artisanal Bread (page 49) is an example. Whole-wheat flour contains the germ and bran of the wheat kernel, which means it is high in fiber, flavor, and nutritional value. Fine-textured cake flour, which is milled from soft wheat that is low in gluten and other proteins, is used for making breads with a tender crumb, such as biscuits.

As the descriptions of these wheat flours indicate, the most important distinction among them is their protein content, specifically gluten. I think of gluten as a bunch of rubber bands that become stretched when the flour is beaten or kneaded, producing an elastic, stretchy dough. That is why dough that has been vigorously beaten or kneaded must usually rest for a short time before it is rolled or patted: the gluten needs to relax a bit so it doesn't "fight" you when you are shaping the dough.

Rye flour is made by grinding grains of rye grass and rye berries. It is low in gluten and is usually combined with a wheat flour to produce a bread that is not too heavy or dense. Rye flour is sold in light, medium, and dark varieties; the varieties differ in how much bran has been left when the flour is milled. Medium and dark rye flours have more flavor than light rye flour. I use medium rye flour in my Dark Rye Bread (page 58).

All the flours I use are available in my local supermarket. I purchase King Arthur brand all-purpose, bread, and whole-wheat flours because the quality is consistently high. When shopping for flour, look for the sell-by date stamped on the bag or box and check on the condition of the packaging. Ideally, the date will be several months in the future and the packaging will show no signs of damage.

Store flours in airtight containers in a cool, dry place. Whole-wheat flour is the exception. It contains the fat-rich germ and should be stored in the refrigerator or, preferably, in the freezer. It is easy to take out only the quantity you need for a recipe, and you will know your flour is always fresh. Spoiled flour will have an unpleasant smell because the oil in the germ will have gone rancid. Storing whole-wheat flour in the freezer also prevents any bug problems. I advise against buying whole-wheat flour or other whole-grain products from the bulk bins in markets, because you don't know how long they have been stored at room temperature.

Flavorings, Spices & Herbs

"Pure" is the word to look for when buying vanilla and almond extracts. Store the extracts tightly capped in a cool, dry cupboard.

Use spices and dried herbs that haven't been on the shelf too long, and store them tightly covered in a cool, dry spot. Storage times vary, and a simple way to check if they are still potent is to put a dab on your finger and taste it. If the spice or herb is no longer fresh, it will have little or no taste and should be discarded. Buy spices and dried herbs in relatively small quantities so you can use them up before their flavor is lost.

Although I usually use supermarket cinnamon to test my recipes, extra-fancy Vietnamese cassia cinnamon (available from Penzeys Spices) is a full-flavored, strong, sweet cinnamon worth trying. Ground black pepper becomes flavorless quickly, so I keep a pepper mill filled with whole peppercorns handy and grind fresh pepper as I need it. For information on salt, see the entry on page 14.

Grain Gains

Mixing grains into bread dough adds both fiber and nutrition. Steel-cut oats, which are the inner portion of oat kernels that have been cut (rather than rolled and steamed like rolled oats), deliver a nutty taste and chewy texture to breads. Old-fashioned rolled oats are a good addition, as well. But I avoid quick-cooking rolled oats and instant oats, because the flakes are too fine.

Wheat bran is the outer layer of the wheat kernel. Oat bran is the outer husk of the oat grain. Both brans are high in fiber. You can add 1 tbsp of either bran to any of the bread recipes to increase the fiber content. It is an easy way to slip in nutrition that is not visible in the finished loaf.

These grains are available in natural foods stores and in the natural foods sections of supermarkets. They should be refrigerated for storage. I buy mine from a natural foods store that keeps its stock of whole grains and brans refrigerated.

Leaveners

The purpose of any leavener is to make breads or other baked goods rise. Air, steam, and yeast are natural leaveners, and baking soda and baking powder are chemical leaveners. When air is beaten into a batter or dough that then goes into a hot oven, the air cells expand in the heat, causing the mass to grow in volume. The same thing happens to the moisture in a dough or batter, which produces steam—water molecules becoming gas—in a hot oven. Air and steam are what cause Very Big Popovers (page 22) and Gruyère & Black Pepper Gougères (page 92) to rise during baking.

When yeast, baking soda, or baking powder are mixed with liquid as part of a batter or dough, carbon dioxide gas cells are produced that cause the batter or dough to rise in the oven. During baking, the gas cells form tiny bubbles or air pockets that set and form the texture—various-sized holes in the crumb—of the finished bread.

Baking soda is an alkaline, or base, that releases carbon dioxide gas only when it is combined with an acidic ingredient, such as sour cream, buttermilk, or molasses. When it is mixed into a moist batter, the baking soda is activated right away and the batter should be promptly baked. Store baking soda in a cool, dry spot; it will keep indefinitely.

Nearly all baking powder available today is "double acting," because it contains baking soda, an alkaline, and two acid ingredients, one of which is activated by liquid and the other by heat. This means that batters and doughs that are leavened with double-acting baking powder do not have to be baked the moment they are mixed, since the second acid does not fully react until it is exposed to the heat of the oven. That said, it is still a good idea not to leave the batter standing for too long—no more than about 5 minutes—before it goes into the oven. As with baking soda, store baking powder in a cool, dry spot. It does not have a long life, however. Check for the expiration date on the bottom of the container, and discard the container when the date has passed.

Yeast is my "relaxed friend" leavening. It is activated by moisture and warmth and produces carbon dioxide gas cells slowly. Yeast doughs have rising periods that give the carbon dioxide gas cells time to form, unlike the gas cells produced by baking soda and baking powder, which appear and dissipate relatively quickly.

A plantlike microorganism, yeast is so tiny that it takes 20 billion yeast cells to make a single gram. It feeds on sugar, ferments, and produces carbon dioxide that is trapped in an elastic bread dough. As the carbon dioxide gas forms, expands, and produces bubbles, the dough inflates, or rises. When you press (punch down) the air out of a risen dough, you are actually pressing out the trapped gases. Sucrose (cane sugar) causes yeast to grow rapidly, and a small amount is often mixed with yeast and water to proof the yeast—in other words, prove that the yeast is viable. Salt, which is added after the proofed yeast is combined with flour, adds flavor to breads and also slows yeast down, tempering its action to avoid an overly quick rise. During baking, heat kills the yeast and the gas bubbles set, giving bread its texture. The texture—close grained or coarse grained, soft or crisp crust or crumb—is also largely defined by the type and amount of liquid (water, milk, melted butter) used in the dough.

I use granular yeast, both active dry yeast and instant yeast. The latter, which has finer granules and acts more quickly than active dry yeast, also goes by the names of rapid rise, quick rise, and fast rise. I use active dry yeast when I am letting a dough rest in the refrigerator overnight and instant yeast for other yeast breads. My preferred brand is SAF, which labels its yeasts Traditional Active Dry Yeast and Gourmet Perfect Rise Yeast, the latter an instant yeast.

Yeast packets carry expiration dates. My experience is that dry, granular yeast is reliable, so I check the date and trust the package and do not proof it. Yeast-package expiration dates are often a year out, so I look for them before I buy yeast and often find fresher packets with more-distant dates in the same display. If you want to check the yeast's viability, simply dissolve a packet in about 3 tbsp lukewarm or warm water (the water feels warm and comfortable when you touch it), add about ¼ tsp granulated sugar, and let the mixture sit for 5 to 10 minutes. The mixture will look a bit foamy and show slight movement as the yeast cells expel carbon dioxide. Then add the dissolved yeast with the liquids in the recipe, rather than mixing it with the dry ingredients as I usually do.

Milk & Buttermilk

The addition of milk to a bread dough produces a softer texture and crust than water does. If I used milk with a particular butterfat content, such as whole milk or low-fat milk, in a recipe, I have specified it in the ingredients list. If not, I have called simply for milk and indicated that any fat content will do.

The buttermilk available in my local markets is nonfat, and that is what I used in the recipes. If the buttermilk available to you has a different fat content, it will work fine.

Nuts

I use blanched almonds (without skins), natural almonds (with skins), blanched or natural sliced almonds, pecans, walnuts, and peeled hazelnuts in the recipes. All of the nuts used in this book are unsalted. New crops of nuts appear in supermarkets from October to December, and this is a good time to buy a year's supply. If the nuts are stored in the freezer in a tightly sealed heavy-duty freezer bag or an airtight plastic freezer container, they will remain in good condition for up to a year. Thaw nuts before using them in recipes. If any nuts are black or wrinkled, discard them. Pecan halves sometimes have small pieces of a bitter shell-like piece attached to the center that should be removed and discarded.

Toasting brings out the flavor in nuts. If they are frozen, thaw them before toasting. Spread all nuts in a single layer on a baking sheet and toast them in a preheated oven. Toast walnuts and pecans at 325°F for 8 to 10 minutes. Toast blanched or natural sliced almonds at 350°F for 12 to 15 minutes, and blanched or natural whole almonds and hazelnuts at 350°F for about 15 minutes. Shake the pan once during toasting to redistribute the nuts so they heat evenly. Watch the nuts closely to prevent burning. Not long before the nuts are ready, a pleasant, toasty aroma should be evident, and all of the nuts will take on color, with the blanched ones turning evenly golden. Some of the oil in hazelnuts rises to the surface during toasting, giving the nuts a sheen.

If you cannot find peeled hazelnuts in the market, you will need to peel them before toasting. Bring a saucepan filled with water to a boil, add the hazelnuts, and blanch for 5 minutes. Drain them in a sieve, and then immerse them in cold water for about 5 minutes to cool. Drain them again and use a small, sharp knife to peel them. The skin slips off easily and the nuts are ready to toast. Any moisture is removed in oven.

Salt

Salt adds flavor to breads and controls the action of yeast. I use kosher salt, which is free of preservatives and has a clear, fresh salt taste. It has a slightly coarse grain, but it goes through my flour sifter and sieve. Look for a salt brand that does not contain an anticaking agent.

Many varieties of sea salt are available, and most of them are a good choice for a salt topping. Sample them until you find one or more you especially like.

Sugars & Other Sweeteners

Sweeteners are important in bread making. Yeast feeds happily on them and then forms the gases that make dough rise, plus they contribute to attractive browned crusts. Granulated sugar, light brown sugar, dark brown sugar, and powdered sugar are used in this book. Store all sugars tightly covered in a clean, dry place. If granulated sugar becomes wet, it dries hard as a rock and cannot be used. Brown sugar is granulated sugar to which molasses has been added for color, with light brown sugar containing less than dark brown sugar. The molasses also makes the sugar naturally moist. I store brown sugar in a sealed plastic bag that is rolled tightly against the sugar to keep it from drying out. Powdered sugar is granulated sugar that has been ground to a powder, with a little cornstarch added to prevent caking.

Light and dark corn syrup, molasses, honey, and maple syrup are my primary liquid sweeteners. I use unsulfured light molasses, which has a milder flavor than sulfured molasses, and pure maple syrup. Avoid maple-flavored syrups, which are typically corn syrup with little or no real maple syrup in the mix.

FILLING THE BREAD PAN

This is a self-guided tour to understanding the process of mixing, shaping, and baking all kinds of breads. Different types call for different mixing methods, but once you know the basic technique for assembling a muffin, biscuit, yeast bread, or other dough or batter, recipes will not only go together more quickly, but you will also be more comfortable making them. The same is true for shaping breads—whether they be loaves, rounds, twists, crescents, swirled buns, or myriad other forms—or for judging doneness—from crumbly scones, sky-high popovers, and crisp bread to tender sandwich loaves. Knowledge is bread power.

Near the beginning of each recipe, I have included approximate times for various steps to help you plan how long it will take to complete the bread. Which steps are included will depend on the recipe. For example, recipes in the Superfast Breads chapter usually include only mixing time and baking temperature and time, but recipes in the Refrigerator Breads chapter often include details for those two steps, plus refrigerator time and rising time.

Mixing time: How long it takes to mix components of a recipe.

Resting time: How long a batter or dough must rest at room temperature.

Refrigerator time: How long a batter or dough can or must rest or chill in the refrigerator.

Rising time: How long a yeast bread will need to rise.

Baking: At what temperature and about how long a bread bakes.

Mixing Breads Made Without Yeast

When mixing muffins, corn breads, pancakes, and waffles, have two bowls ready. Depending on the specific recipe, stir, sift, or whisk the dry ingredients together in one bowl. In the second bowl, whisk or stir together the liquid ingredients. Pour the dry ingredients over the liquid ingredients and mix together with a large spoon just until all the ingredients are combined. When you are mixing these kinds of breads, you are moistening the ingredients, not beating them. Some small lumps will remain in the batter, which will dissolve during baking.

It takes only one bowl to mix popovers. Whisk together the liquid ingredients and salt, and then slowly whisk in the flour just until the ingredients are blended. This batter will also have small lumps.

Biscuits and scones are made with either cold or melted butter or shortening. For a recipe made with cold butter or shortening, sift or whisk together the dry ingredients in a bowl, scatter the butter or shortening (cut into pieces) over the top, and then cut the pieces into the flour with fingertips, a pair of table knives, or a pastry blender until pea-sized pellets of flour and fat form. Add the liquid ingredients to this crumbly mixture and stir to make a soft dough. Pieces of butter or shortening will still be visible, which is what you want, because they will expand in the oven, causing the biscuits or scones to rise. Scrape the dough out of the bowl onto a work surface and knead 5 to 10 strokes to form a smooth, rather than ragged, dough. Pat or roll out the dough and cut into desired shapes. When making biscuits or scones with melted butter or shortening, combine the dry ingredients the same way and stir in the melted butter or shortening with the other liquids to form a soft dough. The kneading, rolling, and cutting remain the same.

Beignets and *gougères* are made with a cream puff dough, known as *pâte à choux*, that uses water for the liquid. There are three stages to making these "breads": stove-top cooking, beating in eggs, and frying or baking. Bring water, butter, and salt to a boil, add the dry ingredients, and stir for a few minutes to cook the flour. Next, beat the dough, and then beat in the eggs. Finally, drop the dough into hot oil to fry or spoon onto a baking sheet and bake in the oven.

Mixing Yeast Breads

Before I explain how to mix yeast breads, I want to emphasize one truth. Using yeast and making a yeast dough is easy. I wish I could write that sentence at least ten times. If you haven't baked with yeast, try one or two of the recipes that use it and you will soon feel comfortable working with it. Yeast is a forgiving ingredient. If the temperature of the liquid you are adding to it or the room temperature is not optimal, yeast will adjust. A dough can take longer to rise if you add cold liquid, or it can rise more quickly than anticipated if the kitchen is warm, but neither factor will ruin your bread. And if your bread is ever "ruined," what have you lost? Only a little flour and water. And if it is a success, what have you gained? The whole house filled with the aroma of bread baking, a huge sense of pride, and the joy of serving and eating something wonderful you have made.

Okay, now that you are ready to bake with yeast, here are the simple guidelines. With only a few exceptions in this book, I have one mixing method for yeast breads. For both active dry yeast and instant yeast, mix the yeast with a portion of the flour and with the other dry ingredients in a large bowl. The liquid—which consists of milk or water, sometimes melted butter, and often a combination of one or more liquids—is heated to about 130°F whether using active dry yeast or instant yeast. If a recipe calls for adding either type of yeast directly to the heated liquid, the liquid should be heated to about 110°F. Liquid at 130°F will feel hot but not burning or uncomfortable to your hand. Liquid at 110°F will feel pleasantly warm. Test the temperature with an instant-read thermometer, feel it, and from then on you can check the temperature by touching the liquid. A few degrees in either direction is fine. Pour the hot liquid over the dry ingredients and mix with an electric mixer or with a large spoon for a couple of minutes. Some recipes will call for covering the bowl with a towel or plastic wrap and letting the dough rest for about 10 minutes. This gives the flour time to absorb some of the liquid and lets the yeast get going in the warm liquid environment.

Add the remaining flour and mix with the mixer or knead by hand, usually for about 5 minutes. If kneading the dough by hand, use a lightly floured flat, smooth work surface. Gather the dough together on the prepared surface. Using the heel of one hand, push the dough down and away against the surface. Then, using your fingertips, fold it toward you. Rotate the dough a quarter turn and repeat the pushing and folding. Continue to repeat until the dough looks smooth and feels supple and elastic.

You can also mix and knead the dough in a food processor, though you will probably have to knead the dough in two or more batches. Kneading in a food processor will only take about 30 seconds. After the last portion of flour is added and incorporated, separate the dough into manageable portions to knead it. Each batch will take only about 30 seconds. As noted in my earlier discussion on the food processor (page 9), however, I have found it is easier to mix and knead by mixer or by hand, than to divide the dough into batches for kneading in a food processor.

All of the yeast breads in this book can be kneaded with the flat beater of a stand mixer except for two, which require the dough hook: Crusty Artisanal Bread (page 49) and Multigrain Crusty Bread (page 52). These breads can be kneaded by hand, as well. If the dough will be formed into rolls or other specific shapes after kneading, it is often a good idea to let it rest for a short time to allow the gluten in the flour to relax.

Shaping Breads

The next step is to shape the dough and put it in or on a pan to rise. If you are making a refrigerator dough, you can delay this step. Put the dough in a buttered, oiled, or floured bowl, cover the bowl with plastic wrap and refrigerate the bowl. How long the dough rests in the refrigerator is up to you and your schedule. All of the refrigerator doughs will keep overnight and usually up to 2 days.

The easiest way to shape round rolls is to roll them between your palms into firm, smooth balls. For crescents, roll out the dough into a circle and cut the circle into wedges. Then, starting at the wide end, roll up each wedge and bend the roll into a crescent shape. For Parker House Rolls (page 60), roll out the dough, cut it into circles, and make a crease near or at the center of each circle. Spread soft butter on the crease and fold the dough over along the crease, pressing the edges to seal.

Loaves made from a soft dough only need to have the dough scraped into the pan. To form a loaf from a firm dough, pat the dough into a square, fold the dough in half, and press the edges to seal. Use your hands to roll and press the dough gently into a loaf shape, tapering the ends slightly. A similar method is used to form an oval loaf, but you will need to roll your hands along the dough from the center out, increasing the pressure as you reach near the ends of the loaf.

Loosely cover any dough left to rise with plastic wrap, a kitchen towel, or waxed paper, depending on the recipe. Covering the dough keeps it moist and soft and creates the warm, humid conditions in which yeast thrives.

Kitchen temperatures affect rising times. The times in the recipes are what were needed when I tested the breads in my kitchen, where the temperature is usually between 65° and 70°F. Properly risen dough will look puffy and have a pleasant sweet, yeasty smell. It will not necessarily double in size. How much a dough "grows" depends on the specific dough. Each recipe describes how a risen dough should look and/or feel.

Slashing Breads

Despite the terminology, this is not a violent act. About 15 minutes before the end of rising, make cuts in the top of a loaf that will bake up into crusty bread. These slashes make it easier for bread to expand and rise evenly during baking. Using a small, sharp knife or single-edge razor blade (hold it carefully and then store it safely), and holding it at a roughly 45-degree angle, quickly make several ¼-in-deep, or slightly deeper, cuts in the top of the bread. For a long loaf, cut a series of three to five diagonal slashes, depending on the length of the loaf; for a round loaf, cut a crisscross, a tic-tac-toe design, a single long slash, or a few parallel lines. Slashing takes a bit of practice, and you will get better at it the more you do it. When you have gained confidence, you can become more creative with your slashes.

Baking & Cooling Breads

Breads made from a liquid batter, such as a tea bread, are done when the top feels firm and a toothpick inserted in the center comes out clean. Popovers are done when they are puffed and browned and have completed their baking time.

Breads are typically done when they reach a certain color, such as golden, lightly browned, or browned, depending on the recipe. Most yeast breads should be firm and will have developed a nice brown crust. As long as the temperature in your oven is accurate (see how to check the accuracy in the oven discussion on page 9), baking times are a good guideline. If you are not sure if a yeast bread is ready, most loaves are not harmed by an additional few minutes of baking, as long as the crust does not burn.

Unless I indicate that a bread can be served warm, you should allow it to cool completely on a wire rack. The rack allows air to circulate around the cooling bread, which prevents condensation that can make it soggy.

ANYTIME FRESH BREAD

You can't always eat bread the day you bake it, so here are tips on how to store—both at room temperature and in the freezer—and reheat your prized homemade breads so they are always served at their best.

I have a supply of large plastic bread bags that I order from King Arthur Flour to use for storing breads that do not have a crisp crust and for freezing breads. For breads with a crisp crust, I slip the completely cooled loaves into clean brown paper bags, as plastic bags would soften the crust. If bread has been cut, I put plastic wrap over the cut surface, secure it with a rubber band, and store the bread in a brown paper bag at room temperature. My wrapped bread sits on my kitchen counter. A bread box is also useful for bread storage. I wrap and freeze any bread that will not be used within the times specified in the recipes.

If the crisp crust of a bread has softened and the bread has not been cut, it can be warmed, uncovered, in a preheated slow oven (usually 275°F) to crisp the crust. If you want to warm up biscuits, corn bread and corn muffins, rolls, sweet breads, or loaves for serving, cover them with aluminum foil and heat them in an oven preheated to the same temperature used for crisping for about 15 minutes.

With the exception of popovers, pancakes, spoon bread, and any of the fried breads, all of the breads in this book can be frozen. I am not a big fan of freezing bread dough. Frozen dough takes a long time to thaw and then needs more time to rise and bake. It is much easier to bake the bread, freeze it, and have the bread ready to thaw and serve.

To freeze any bread, first make sure it is thoroughly cooled. Wrap large or small breads separately in plastic wrap, and then seal in a plastic freezer bag or wrap in aluminum foil. That extra layer of plastic wrap makes a big difference. It protects the bread from the freezer air and the undesirable flavors it can add to bread. Mark bread wrappers with the date and contents and freeze the bread for up to 3 months. Thaw the bread at room temperature in its wrapper, so that any condensation forms on the wrapper, not the bread.

CHAPTER 01
SUPERFAST BREADS

SUPERFAST BREADS

I have two ways of dealing with an unplanned empty bread basket. One is to check the bread stash in my freezer, and the second is to whip up one of these breads. Although all of the recipes in this book are fast to mix, the breads in this chapter can be mixed in ten minutes or less and do not call for yeast, so there is no rising time. I can mix and then bake these breads while I am getting the rest of a meal together. In the case of Christmas Morning Belgian Waffles (page 34) or Pumpkin-Chocolate Chip Pancakes (page 33), it *is* the meal, whether it is break-fast or supper.

Most of the breads in this chapter can be stirred together by hand. Forming them is as easy as dropping biscuit dough from a spoon, patting scone dough into shape, scraping bread dough into a pan, or pouring popover batter into baking cups.

If you're like me and never seem to have enough hours in the day (or night), this chapter of my tried-and-true speediest bread recipes is for you. These recipes are also a good choice for home cooks who are making their first foray into bread baking—and for filling any bread basket.

BUTTER DROP BISCUITS

INGREDIENTS

> 6 tbsp unsalted butter

> 1½ cups unbleached
all-purpose flour

> ¼ cup cake flour

> 1 tbsp granulated sugar

> 2 tsp baking powder

> 1 tsp baking soda

> 1 tsp kosher salt

> ¼ cup cold shortening,
cut into pieces

> 1 cup cold buttermilk,
any fat content

YIELD
Makes 6 biscuits

MIXING TIME
5 minutes

BAKING
475°F for about 12 minutes

Easy, foolproof, soft, and tender is what I am always looking for in a biscuit, and these fit the bill. They were literally dropped on my doorstep, or actually in my mailbox. Joe Yonan, food editor of the *Washington Post*, put together a biscuit story that included Terry Yonan Beasley's (Joe's sister) fluffy Southern biscuits. The soft dough is dropped into a pan of melted butter, and the result is a tender, butter-coated biscuit. Joe included them in his book *The Fearless Chef*, but generously let me share them here.

METHOD Position a rack in the middle of the oven and preheat to 475°F.

In a heavy, 9-in ovenproof frying pan, melt the butter over low heat. Set aside.

Sift both flours, the sugar, baking powder, baking soda, and salt into a large bowl. Scatter the shortening over the top. Using your thumb and fingertips, two table knives, or a pastry blender, work the shortening into the flour mixture until flour-coated pea-sized pieces form. There will still be some loose flour. Make a well in the center, pour the buttermilk into the well, and use a large spoon to mix the buttermilk into the dry ingredients to form a soft dough.

Using a ¼-cup capacity ice cream scoop or the large spoon, drop 6 rounded scoops of dough into the prepared pan, spacing them about ½ in apart (drop 5 biscuits in a circle around the edge of the pan and 1 biscuit in the middle). Using the large spoon, carefully turn over each biscuit to coat both sides with butter.

Bake until the tops are golden, about 12 minutes. Serve warm, directly from the pan.

The biscuits can be baked up to 3 hours ahead and left in the pan, covered loosely with aluminum foil. To serve, preheat the oven to 275°F and reheat the covered biscuits until warm, about 10 minutes.

VERY BIG POPOVERS

INGREDIENTS

> Flavorless nonstick cooking spray
  for muffin wells

> 3 large eggs

> 1½ cups milk, any fat content

> ¾ tsp kosher salt

> 1½ cups unbleached all-purpose flour

> Butter and jam or Blueberry
  Sauce (page 141) for serving

YIELD
Makes 6 popovers

MIXING TIME
5 minutes

REFRIGERATOR TIME
20 minutes to 2 hours

BAKING
425°F for about 45 minutes,
plus 10 minutes' resting time in oven

My mother-in-law was not a baker, but if she saw a recipe she liked, she would give it to me to make. I tried these popovers for her and the recipe became my never-fail, treasured formula for high-rising popovers. The best way to eat one is to make a slit in the top, drop in butter and jam (strawberry and seedless raspberry are good), and then pull it apart—watch your shirt; the popover will be dripping with melted butter and jam—to eat it. Although they look fragile, once baked, these popovers are quite stable, so they can be kept hot in a turned-off oven for up to 30 minutes.

I bake the popovers in a "Texas" muffin tin (also known as a jumbo muffin tin) that I found in my local supermarket. It has wells with a 1-cup capacity. You can also use a popover pan or heatproof glass or ceramic custard cups with ¾- to 1-cup capacity. If using custard cups, place them on a rimmed baking sheet for easy transport.

Note that the popovers go into a cold oven, and then the oven is immediately turned on.

METHOD Position a rack in the middle of the oven. Have ready a rimmed baking sheet. Generously spray six wells in a jumbo muffin tin (or use one of the alternative baking containers suggested in the introductory note) with flavorless nonstick cooking spray.

continued ↘

VERY BIG POPOVERS

continued ↘

In a large bowl, whisk together the eggs, milk, and salt until blended. Slowly whisk in the flour just until incorporated. The batter will have small lumps of flour but no large globs. Tap the whisk lightly on the side of the bowl if the flour clumps in the wires. Cover and refrigerate the batter for 20 minutes or up to 2 hours.

Pour the batter into a measuring pitcher to make filling the muffin tin easier. Put the prepared muffin tin on the baking sheet. Using a scant ½ cup batter for each popover, pour the batter into the prepared wells. The batter should be at least ¼ in from the rim of each well.

Put the baking sheet in the oven, and immediately turn on the oven to 425°F. Bake until the tops and exposed edges are browned, about 45 minutes. The popovers will rise high over the tops of the cups. Turn off the oven. Using a toothpick, puncture the risen sides in each popover in three places, and let the popovers sit in the turned-off oven with the oven door closed for 10 minutes. This releases some of the steam in the popovers.

Remove as many popovers as needed for a first serving, and leave the remaining ones in the oven for up to 30 minutes to keep warm. Serve with butter and jam.

SAVORY LEMON-LEEK LOAF

INGREDIENTS

> 1 tbsp unsalted butter

> 2 cups chopped leeks, white and light green parts only (about 3 leeks)

> 2 cups unbleached all-purpose flour

> ½ tsp baking soda

> ½ tsp baking powder

> ½ tsp kosher salt

> 4 large eggs

> 1½ cups sour cream

> 1 tbsp grated lemon zest

> ½ tsp freshly ground black pepper

YIELD
Makes 1 loaf

MIXING TIME
10 minutes

BAKING
375°F for about 50 minutes

When my friend Carol Witham brought this bread to a dinner party, I thought it was a yeast bread. I was surprised to discover it was leavened with baking powder and baking soda. It makes a nice accompaniment to most main dishes, especially fish. The leeks, which are cooked in a little butter, add a mild onion flavor to the bread, and the grated lemon zest imparts a fresh citrus taste.

METHOD Position a rack in the middle of the oven and preheat to 375°F. Butter a 9-by-5-by-3-in loaf pan (or any loaf pan with an 8-cup capacity). Line the bottom of the pan with parchment paper and butter the paper.

In a frying pan over medium heat, melt the butter. Add the leeks and cook, stirring often, until softened, about 5 minutes. Remove from the heat.

In a medium bowl, stir together the flour, baking soda, baking powder, and salt. Set aside.

In a large bowl, whisk the eggs until blended. Using a large spoon, stir in the sour cream, leeks with any pan liquid, lemon zest, and pepper. Add the flour mixture and stir until blended and a sticky dough forms. Scrape the dough into the prepared pan.

Bake until the top feels firm and is golden brown, about 50 minutes. Let cool in the pan on a wire rack for about 15 minutes. Run a small, sharp knife around the inside edge of the pan to loosen the bread sides, then turn the bread out onto the rack. Let cool completely before serving.

The bread can be covered and stored at room temperature for 1 day. It is good toasted or cooked with a filling in a panini grill.

CHOICES Stir 1 cup shredded Cheddar cheese, ½ cup crumbled blue cheese, or ½ cup grated Parmesan cheese into the batter with the sour cream.

BOTTOMS-UP CINNAMON-CARAMEL PINWHEELS

INGREDIENTS

Glaze
> 4 tbsp unsalted butter
> 2 tbsp honey
> ½ cup packed light brown sugar

Biscuit Dough
> 1½ cups unbleached all-purpose flour
> ½ cup cake flour
> 1 tbsp granulated sugar
> 1 tsp baking powder
> ½ tsp baking soda
> ¾ tsp kosher salt
> 6 tbsp unsalted butter, melted
> 1 cup sour cream
> ¼ cup buttermilk, any fat content

This is the fast version of a sticky bun. Spread a brown sugar glaze in the bottom of a pan, pat out a soft biscuit dough, roll up the dough with cinnamon sugar, and bake it. Then feast on the fastest, stickiest, cinnamon-swirl buns around.

METHOD Position a rack in the middle of the oven and preheat to 350°F. Line a 9-in round pan or baking dish with 2-in-high sides with parchment paper.

Make the glaze. In a medium saucepan, combine the butter, honey, and brown sugar over medium heat and cook, stirring often, until the butter and sugar melt and the glaze is smooth. Pour the glaze into the prepared pan, tilting the pan to spread it evenly over the bottom. Set aside.

Make the biscuit dough. Sift together both flours, the sugar, baking powder, baking soda, and salt into a medium bowl. Put about half of the flour mixture into a large bowl. Add the butter, sour cream, and buttermilk to the flour mixture in the large bowl and stir with a large spoon until blended. Add the remaining flour mixture to the large bowl and stir until it is incorporated and a soft, ragged dough forms.

With floured hands, gather up the dough and put it on a lightly floured work surface. Knead the dough about 10 strokes: push down and away with the heel of your hand against the surface, then fold the dough in half toward you, and rotate it a quarter turn, flouring the surface as necessary to prevent sticking. The dough is ready when it looks fairly smooth, feels very soft, and there is no loose flour. Pat the dough into a rectangle about 12 by 7 in and ⅜ in thick.

Make the topping. In a small bowl, stir together the sugar and cinnamon. Using a pastry brush, spread the butter evenly over the dough, leaving a 1-in border uncovered on all sides. Sprinkle the cinnamon sugar evenly over the butter.

continued ↘

BOTTOMS-UP CINNAMON-CARAMEL PINWHEELS

Topping

> ¼ cup granulated sugar

> 1 tsp ground cinnamon

> 1 tbsp unsalted butter, melted

....

YIELD
Makes 9 rolls

MIXING TIME
15 minutes

BAKING
350°F for about 25 minutes

continued ↘

Using a thin, metal spatula to help lift the dough, and starting from a long side, roll up the dough, jelly-roll style, pressing the seam to seal. If any dough sticks to the surface, use the spatula to spread the dough back onto the dough cylinder. Pinch the ends to seal. The roll will be about 11 in long. Using a sharp knife, cut the cylinder crosswise into 9 rolls, each about 1¼ in thick. Place them, with a cut side up, in the prepared pan, arranging 7 rolls around the edge of the pan and 2 rolls in the middle. Pinch together any edges that separate.

Bake until the tops feel firm and the edges just start to brown, about 25 minutes. Let cool in the pan on a wire rack for 5 minutes. Turn out onto a serving plate and peel away the parchment. Serve warm.

The pinwheels can be baked 1 day ahead, unmolded as directed, covered, and left at room temperature. To serve, preheat the oven to 275°F and reheat the pinwheels, sticky side up, until warm, about 15 minutes.

CHOICES Sprinkle ⅓ cup raisins or dried cranberries over the cinnamon sugar.

TOASTED PECAN & CHOCOLATE CHUNK SCONES

INGREDIENTS

> 2 cups unbleached all-purpose flour
> ¼ cup granulated sugar
> 1¼ tsp baking powder
> ¼ tsp baking soda
> ¼ tsp kosher salt
> ½ cup cold unsalted butter,
>   cut into 16 pieces
> ⅔ cup buttermilk, any fat content
> 2 tbsp pure maple syrup
> 3 oz semisweet chocolate, chopped
> ½ cup pecans, toasted (see page 13)
>   and coarsely chopped
> 1 large egg lightly beaten with 1 tbsp
>   heavy cream for egg wash
> Vanilla whipped cream (page 141)
>   for serving (optional)

YIELD
Makes 8 scones

MIXING TIME
10 minutes

BAKING
400°F for about 18 minutes

I discovered what a good baker my friend Carol Witham was when she served these scones at a tea party. They are laced with warm, soft pieces of melted chocolate and crunchy toasted pecans. Serve them with raspberry jam and butter, or with clotted cream for an over-the-top scone experience.

METHOD Position a rack in the middle of the oven and preheat to 400°F. Line a baking sheet with parchment paper.

In a large bowl, whisk together the flour, sugar, baking powder, baking soda, and salt. Scatter the butter pieces over the top. Using your thumb and fingertips, two table knives, or a pastry blender, work the butter into the flour mixture until flour-coated pea-sized pieces form. There will still be some loose flour. Make a well in the center, pour the buttermilk and maple syrup into the well, and use a large spoon to mix them into the dry ingredients to form a soft dough. Stir in the chocolate and pecans.

With floured hands, gather up the dough and put it on a lightly floured work surface. Knead the dough about 5 strokes: push down and away with the heel of your hand against the surface, then fold the dough in half toward you, and rotate it a quarter turn, flouring the surface as necessary to prevent sticking. The dough is ready when it looks smooth, feels soft, and there is no loose flour. Lightly flour the work surface again and pat the dough into a 7-in circle 1¼ in thick. Cut the circle into 8 wedges by cutting it into quarters and then cutting the quarters in half. Use a wide spatula to transfer the scones to the prepared baking sheet, spacing them about 1½ in apart. Using a pastry brush, brush the tops with the egg wash. (You will not use all of the egg wash).

Bake until the tops are lightly browned and the bottoms are browned, about 18 minutes. Transfer to a wire rack to cool for at least 15 minutes before serving. Accompany with whipped cream, if desired.

The scones can be baked 1 day ahead, covered, and stored at room temperature. To serve, preheat the oven to 275°F and reheat the scones until warm, about 15 minutes.

CHERRY & ALMOND WHOLE-WHEAT SCONES

INGREDIENTS

> 1½ cups unbleached all-purpose flour

> ½ cup whole-wheat flour

> ½ cup granulated sugar, plus 2 tsp

> 1 tsp baking powder

> 1 tsp baking soda

> ½ tsp kosher salt

> 1 tsp ground cinnamon

> 1 tsp grated orange zest

> ½ cup cold unsalted butter, cut into 16 pieces

A bit of whole-wheat flour for flavor and fiber, always-in-season dried cherries, and a sweet crunchy almond topping make these scones worth trying. Although the outside bakes up crisp, the dough is quite soft and can be patted out rather than rolled. A soft dough makes the inside of the scone especially moist and tender. These scones will spread quite a bit during baking, so be sure to give them adequate space on the pan.

METHOD Position a rack in the middle of the oven and preheat to 400°F. Line a baking sheet with parchment paper.

In a large bowl, whisk together both flours, the ½ cup sugar, the baking powder, baking soda, salt, and cinnamon. Stir in the orange zest. Scatter the butter pieces over the top. Using your thumb and fingertips, two table knives, or a pastry blender, work the butter into the flour mixture until flour-coated pea-sized pieces form. There will still be some loose flour. Make a well in the center, add the buttermilk, vanilla, almond extract, and cherries to the well, and use a large spoon to mix them into the dry ingredients to form a soft dough.

With floured hands, gather the dough into a soft ball, put it on a floured rolling surface, and pat into an 8-in circle about ¾ in thick. Cut the circle into 8 wedges by cutting it into quarters and then cutting the quarters in half. Use a wide spatula to transfer the scones to the prepared baking sheet, placing them about 3 in apart. Using a pastry brush, brush the tops with the egg wash. (You will not use all of the egg wash). Sprinkle the almonds evenly over the top, pressing them gently onto the dough. Sprinkle the remaining 2 tsp sugar over the nuts.

continued ↘

CHERRY & ALMOND
WHOLE-WHEAT SCONES

- > 1 tsp pure vanilla extract
- > ½ tsp pure almond extract
- > ¾ cup buttermilk, any fat content
- > ½ cup dried pitted cherries
- > 1 large egg, lightly beaten, for egg wash
- > 3 tbsp natural or blanched sliced almonds or coarsely chopped natural almonds
- > Cherry jam and butter or clotted cream for serving

YIELD
Makes 8 scones

MIXING TIME
10 minutes

BAKING
400°F for about 15 minutes

continued ↘

Bake until the tops are lightly colored, the edges are lightly browned, and the bottoms are browned, about 15 minutes. Transfer to a wire rack to cool for at least 15 minutes before serving. Accompany with jam and butter.

The scones can be baked 1 day ahead, covered, and left at room temperature. To serve, preheat the oven to 275°F and reheat the scones until warm, about 15 minutes.

PUMPKIN-CHOCOLATE CHIP PANCAKES

INGREDIENTS

> 1 cup unbleached all-purpose flour

> 1 tsp baking powder

> ½ tsp baking soda

> ¼ tsp kosher salt

> 1 tsp ground cinnamon

> ½ tsp ground ginger

> ¾ cup milk, any fat content

> 1 large egg

> 3 tbsp pure maple syrup

> ¾ cup canned pumpkin

> ¼ cup full-fat or low-fat plain yogurt

> ⅔ cup semisweet chocolate chips, or 4½ oz semisweet chocolate, chopped

> 2 tbsp unsalted butter

> 1 cup vanilla yogurt for serving

YIELD
Makes twelve 4-in pancakes

MIXING TIME
10 minutes

COOKING
4½ to 6 minutes per batch

I have never understood pancake mixes. Homemade pancake batter is fast and easy to mix and allows so many interesting variations. These pancakes, which are a rich pumpkin color, are sweetened with maple syrup, spiced with cinnamon and ginger, and include warm chocolate chips in every bite.

METHOD Sift together the flour, baking powder, baking soda, salt, cinnamon, and ginger into a medium bowl. Make a well in the center and add the milk, egg, maple syrup, pumpkin, and plain yogurt to the well. Using a large spoon, stir the batter just until all the ingredients are blended and there is no loose flour. You may see some small lumps; that's okay. Stir in the chocolate chips just until evenly distributed.

Preheat the oven to 250° F. You will be keeping the first batches of pancakes warm in the oven until all the batter is used.

Heat a griddle or large frying pan over medium heat, and add 1 tbsp of the butter. Using a pastry brush (preferably silicone), spread the butter evenly over the surface. Using 3 tbsp for each pancake, ladle the batter onto the hot griddle, being careful not to crowd the pancakes. After 3 to 4 minutes, when bubbles have formed near the edges of the pancakes (they will not bubble in the center), the edges have begun to look dry, and the underside is golden brown, carefully turn the pancakes with a spatula. Cook until lightly browned on the second sides, 1½ to 2 minutes longer. Transfer to an ovenproof platter in a single layer and place in the oven. Do not cover the pancakes or they will become get soggy. Repeat with the remaining batter, adding additional butter to the griddle as needed.

Serve the pancakes hot and pass the vanilla yogurt at the table.

CHOICES Omit the chocolate chips and serve with warmed pure maple syrup. Or, omit the chocolate chips and stir ¾ cup pecan or walnut pieces, toasted (see page 13), into the batter; accompany with warmed pure maple syrup.

CHRISTMAS MORNING BELGIAN WAFFLES

INGREDIENTS

> Flavorless nonstick cooking spray or corn or canola oil for waffle iron

> 2 cups unbleached all-purpose flour

> 2½ tsp baking powder

> ¾ tsp baking soda

> ½ tsp salt

> 4 large eggs, separated

> 1½ cups whole milk

> 1 cup full-fat or low-fat plain yogurt

> ½ cup unsalted butter, melted

> 2 tbsp pure maple syrup

> Toppings of choice for serving

YIELD

Makes sixteen 4-in square waffles

MIXING TIME

10 minutes

COOKING

About 3 minutes per batch

For several years, my friend Maureen Egan and her family have invited me to share their Christmas morning and these special waffles, which are easy to put together and are the lightest and crispest waffles I have ever eaten. They are so good that they don't even need syrup, but I admit that plain yogurt, whipped cream (see page 141), fresh berries, or a combination of toppings is mighty good, too. Served with bacon or sausages and fruit, the waffles also make a nice Sunday supper.

I prefer a Belgian-style waffle iron, which has larger indentations than ordinary irons do. It makes for crispier edges and a nice, soft interior.

METHOD Spray a waffle iron with flavorless nonstick cooking spray or brush lightly with oil. Preheat the waffle iron according to the manufacturer's directions. Preheat the oven to 250°F. You will be keeping the cooked waffles warm in the oven until all the batter is used.

Sift together the flour, baking powder, baking soda, and salt into a medium bowl. In a large bowl, whisk together the egg yolks, milk, yogurt, melted butter, and maple syrup until blended. A few bits of melted butter may firm up; that's okay. In a spotlessly clean large bowl, using an electric mixer on medium-high speed, beat the egg whites until firm peaks form.

Stir the flour mixture into the egg yolk mixture just until combined. Using a rubber spatula, fold the egg whites into the batter just until no white specks are visible.

Ladle enough batter evenly onto the hot waffle iron to fill it, according to the manufacturer's directions. My iron calls for a generous ⅓ cup for each waffle. Close the waffle iron and cook until the waffles are browned, about 3 minutes. The waffles are ready if, when you lift the top of the waffle iron, the waffle releases easily from it. Also, the steam escaping from the seam of the iron will have subsided. Transfer to an ovenproof platter and keep warm in the oven. Repeat to cook the remaining batter.

Serve the waffles hot with one or more toppings of choice.

CHAPTER 02
CORN BREADS

CORN BREADS

Poised to set the country on fire; steeped in tradition, performing tirelessly; powerful, creating . . . an unrivaled experience—these are publicity phrases used to describe Cornmeal, the bluegrass band. But they could just as well be describing cornmeal used for baking, especially if they are talking about the nutrition-rich, good-tasting stone-ground cornmeal used for the muffins, breads, corn sticks, and other recipes in this chapter.

The traditional method for producing cornmeal is to grind dried corn between large millstones into a fine, medium, or coarse grind, with much of the nutrition- and flavor-packed hull and germ retained. The modern method of grinding the kernels between huge steel rollers removes virtually all of the hull and germ, and with them, most of the flavor and nearly all of the nutrition. Those facts make the choice of stone-ground cornmeal an easy one.

With the exception of Spoon Bread (page 46), all of these corn breads are mixed by hand. The idea is to mix the ingredients together just enough to moisten the batter. Vigorous or prolonged stirring develops the gluten in the flour portion of the batter, which can toughen and coarsen the texture and can sometimes cause large holes, known as tunnels, to form. Some small lumps in a cornmeal batter are fine, but you don't want big globs of dry ingredients.

Many of these corn breads are served warm from the oven. They can also be made ahead and reheated. Whenever you reheat them, always cover them loosely with aluminum foil to keep them moist.

BACON & CHEDDAR CORN BREAD

INGREDIENTS

> 1 cup unbleached all-purpose flour

> ¼ cup granulated sugar

> 2 tsp baking powder

> 1 tsp baking soda

> ½ tsp kosher salt

> 1¼ cups fine- or medium-grind stone-
ground yellow cornmeal

> 1½ cups buttermilk, any fat content

> 1 large egg

> 2 tbsp unsalted butter, melted

> 4 thick slices bacon
(about 5 oz total), fried crisp, drained,
and broken into small pieces

> 1 cup shredded Cheddar cheese

YIELD
Makes one 9-in square loaf

MIXING TIME
10 minutes

BAKING
400°F for about 20 minutes

Crisp bacon pieces dot this corn bread with good bacon flavor, and small chunks of cheese melt into the bread, making it exceptionally moist. The combination makes a good accompaniment to breakfast, brunch, a lunchtime salad, or a barbecue dinner—or any time of day.

METHOD Position a rack in the middle of the oven and preheat to 400°F. Butter a 9-in square pan with 2-in sides.

Sift together the flour, sugar, baking powder, baking soda, and salt into a medium bowl. Stir in the cornmeal and set aside. In a large bowl, using a fork, stir together the buttermilk, egg, and melted butter until blended. Pour the flour mixture over the buttermilk mixture and use a large spoon to stir the batter slowly just to combine the ingredients. You will see some small lumps; that's okay. Stir in the bacon and cheese. Scrape into the prepared pan.

Bake until the top feels firm if lightly touched and a toothpick inserted in the center comes out clean, about 20 minutes. Let cool in the pan on a wire rack for about 10 minutes, then cut into squares and serve warm.

The corn bread can be baked a day ahead, covered, and left at room temperature. To serve, preheat the oven to 275°F and reheat the bread, covered, until warm, about 15 minutes.

BUTTERMILK CORN BREAD

INGREDIENTS

> 1 tbsp unsalted butter,
  plus 4 tbsp melted butter

> 1 cup unbleached all-purpose flour

> ⅓ cup granulated sugar

> 2 tsp baking powder

> 1 tsp baking soda

> ½ tsp kosher salt

> 1 cup fine-grind stone-ground
  yellow cornmeal

> 1¼ cups buttermilk, any fat content

> 1 large egg

YIELD
Makes one 8-in square bread

MIXING TIME
10 minutes

BAKING
400°F for about 20 minutes

I lose control when I make this corn bread. After the bread has been out of the oven for just a few minutes, I can't help cutting a square (that first piece is a corner piece, with two crisp, buttery sides) and slathering it with soft butter that melts immediately. And for me, it never stops with just one square.

I prefer fine-grind cornmeal for this recipe, but medium grind will also work. The corn bread is used for BLT Corn Bread Salad (page 127).

METHOD Position a rack in the middle of the oven and preheat to 400°F. Put the 1 tbsp butter in an 8-in square pan with 2-in sides. About 2 minutes before you are ready to pour the batter into the pan, put the pan in the preheated oven to melt the butter.

Sift together the flour, sugar, baking powder, baking soda, and salt into a medium bowl. Stir in the cornmeal and set aside. In a large bowl, using a fork, stir together the buttermilk, egg, and the 4 tbsp melted butter until blended. Pour the flour mixture over the buttermilk mixture and use a large spoon to stir the batter slowly just to combine the ingredients. You will see some small lumps; that's okay.

Remove the pan from the oven and tilt it to coat the bottom and sides with the melted butter. The butter may be browned (this is fine), but should not be burnt. Scrape the batter into the prepared pan.

Bake until the top feels firm if lightly touched and a toothpick inserted in the center comes out clean, about 20 minutes. Let cool in the pan on a wire rack for about 10 minutes (if you can), then cut into squares and serve warm.

The corn bread can be baked a day ahead, covered, and left at room temperature. To serve, preheat the oven to 275°F and reheat the bread, covered, until warm, about 15 minutes.

SOUTHERN CORN STICKS

INGREDIENTS

> 2 tsp unsalted butter, melted

> 1 tsp corn or canola oil plus 1 tbsp

> 2 tbsp unbleached all-purpose flour

> ¾ cup fine-grind stoneground
> yellow cornmeal

> 1 tbsp granulated sugar

> ½ tsp baking powder

> ½ tsp baking soda

> ¼ tsp kosher salt

> ½ cup buttermilk, any fat content

> 1 large egg

YIELD
Makes 7 corn sticks

MIXING TIME
10 minutes

BAKING
425°F for about 15 minutes

When I was growing up in Florida, we often had dinner at Morrison's cafeteria. My favorite part of the outing was reaching the end of the line where the hot corn sticks were served. They were crisp on the outside and soft on the inside and were topped with pats of butter that melted over them. The cafeteria is long gone, but not the corn sticks. They survive in this recipe.

Most recipes for corn sticks call for a large proportion of cornmeal to flour. That ratio and baking the batter in a hot, well-greased heavy pan with long, narrow corn-shaped openings are what produce the crisp exterior on corn sticks. Southerners pass down well-seasoned pans from generation to generation; other cooks can find them in most cookware stores. Traditional pans are made of cast iron and usually have seven openings.

METHOD Position a rack in the middle of the oven and preheat to 425°F. Have ready a heavyweight corn stick pan with seven openings.

In a small pan, melt the butter with the 1 tsp of oil. Use a pastry brush to brush the corn stick pan openings generously with the butter-oil mixture. Heat the pan in the oven for 5 minutes while you mix the batter.

In a large bowl, stir together the flour, cornmeal, sugar, baking powder, baking soda, and salt. Add the buttermilk, egg, and the remaining 1 tbsp oil and use a large spoon to stir the batter slowly just to combine the ingredients. You will see some small lumps; that's okay.

Remove the pan from the oven and spoon about 2 tbsp of the batter into each opening. The batter will fill to the rim.

continued ↘

SOUTHERN CORN STICKS

continued ↘

Bake until the tops are lightly browned and a toothpick inserted in the center of a corn stick comes out clean, about 15 minutes. The bottoms of the corn sticks will be browned. Let cool in the pan on a wire rack for 5 minutes. Use a small, sharp knife and your fingers to loosen the edges of the sticks and carefully remove the sticks from the pan to the rack. Do not want to turn the pan upside down to release the corn sticks because it could weigh them down and break them. Serve warm.

The corn sticks can be baked a day ahead, covered, and left at room temperature. To serve, preheat the oven to 275°F and reheat the sticks, uncovered, until warm, about 10 minutes.

APRICOT CORN MUFFINS

INGREDIENTS

> 1 cup fine-grind stone-ground yellow cornmeal
> 1 cup unbleached all-purpose flour
> 1 tsp baking powder
> 1 tsp baking soda
> ½ tsp kosher salt
> ½ cup whole milk
> 6 tbsp unsalted butter, melted
> ⅓ cup pure maple syrup
> 2 large eggs
> ½ cup dried apricots, coarsely chopped
> Butter for serving

YIELD
Makes 6 large muffins

MIXING TIME
10 minutes

BAKING
375°F for about 20 minutes

Brown and crusty all over the outside and soft and moist inside are what I look for in a good corn muffin. Add dried apricot pieces for a chewy, sweet, tart surprise and you have the ideal corn muffin. Kitchen scissors make quick work of cutting the apricots into small pieces.

METHOD Position a rack in the middle of the oven and preheat to 375°F. Butter six wells (each with 1-cup capacity) in a jumbo muffin tin.

In a medium bowl, stir together the cornmeal, flour, baking powder, baking soda, and salt. In a large bowl, using a fork, stir together the milk, butter, maple syrup, and eggs until blended. Stir in the apricot pieces. Pour the flour mixture over the milk mixture, and use a large spoon to stir the batter slowly just to combine the ingredients. You will see some small lumps; that's okay. You will have 3 cups batter. Pour ½ cup batter into each prepared muffin well.

Bake until the tops feel firm if lightly touched and are evenly browned (signaling the sides are browned) and a toothpick inserted in the center of a muffin comes out clean, about 20 minutes. Let cool in the pan on a wire rack for about 10 minutes. Run a small, sharp knife around the inside edge of each well to loosen the muffin sides, then turn the muffins out onto the rack to cool for at least 15 minutes. Serve warm or at room temperature with butter.

The muffins can be baked up to 2 days ahead, covered, and left at room temperature. To serve, preheat the oven to 275°F and reheat the muffins, covered, until warm, about 10 minutes.

CHOICES You can use this recipe to make 12 standard muffins. Use a standard muffin tin with wells with ½-cup capacity. Use ¼ cup batter for each muffin, and start checking to see if the muffins are ready after 15 minutes of baking.

HUSH PUPPIES

Hush puppies are actually cornmeal fritters seasoned with onion and sometimes garlic. According to legend, this Southern specialty originated when a cook was frying up supper and the family dog began yelping. To quiet the dog, the cook threw it some fried cornmeal batter and then said, "Hush, puppy!" My advice is to skip feeding the dog and eat the hot and crispy hush puppies yourself.

METHOD In a large bowl, stir together the cornmeal, flour, baking soda, and salt. Stir in the buttermilk and egg just to moisten and blend the ingredients. Stir in the onion.

Line a baking sheet with paper towels and place near the stove. Pour 2 in of oil into a heavy, medium saucepan and heat over medium heat to 365°F on a deep-frying thermometer. Using a large spoon, drop the batter by tablespoons into the hot oil, frying 6 or 7 at a time. The batter will puff and float to the top. Fry until the undersides are browned, about 2 minutes. Using a slotted spoon, turn and fry on the second sides until a deep golden brown, about 2 minutes longer. Using the slotted spoon, transfer to the towel-lined pan to drain. Fry the remaining batter the same way in two batches, allowing the oil to return to 365°F before adding each batch.

Sprinkle lightly with salt and serve immediately.

INGREDIENTS

> 1 cup fine- or medium-grind stone-ground yellow cornmeal
> ½ cup unbleached all-purpose flour
> 1½ tsp baking soda
> ½ tsp kosher salt
> 1 cup buttermilk, any fat content
> 1 large egg, lightly beaten
> 1 medium yellow onion, finely chopped
> Corn oil for deep-frying
> Kosher or sea salt for finishing

YIELD
Makes about 20 fritters

MIXING TIME
10 minutes

FRYING
About 4 minutes per batch at 365°F.

SPOON BREAD

INGREDIENTS

> 1 cup fine-grind stone-ground yellow cornmeal

> 2 cups water

> 3 tbsp unsalted butter, at room temperature

> 4 large eggs

> 1 tsp kosher salt

> 1 cup whole milk

> 1 tsp baking powder

> Butter for serving

YIELD
Makes 8 servings

MIXING TIME
15 minutes

BAKING
350°F for about 1 hour

This Southern specialty is somewhat like a corn bread soufflé. Many spoon bread recipes call for beaten egg whites, but I have found that beating whole eggs for a couple of minutes produces an equally light result. This recipe goes together easily: you cook cornmeal with water until it thickens and then you beat it into the liquid ingredients. Leftovers will not regain their light texture, but they will make a comforting breakfast "porridge": warm, covered, in a slow oven (about 275°F) and serve topped with butter.

METHOD Position a rack in the middle of the oven and preheat to 350°F. Butter a soufflé or other round baking dish with a 2-qt capacity.

In a large, heavy saucepan, combine the cornmeal and water, place over medium heat, and bring to a simmer, whisking constantly. Cook, whisking constantly, until the mixture thickens, about 3 minutes, then continue to whisk for 1 minute. There should be only an occasional bubble and never a full boil. Remove from the heat and whisk in the butter. It will melt quickly. Scrape the batter into a large bowl and let cool slightly.

In another large bowl, using a stand mixer fitted with the flat beater, beat together the eggs and salt on medium speed for 2 minutes. On low speed, mix in the milk and baking powder. Slowly add large spoonfuls (about 5 additions) of the cornmeal mixture to the batter, incorporating each addition before adding the next one. The batter will be thin and there will be a few small lumps. Scrape into the prepared soufflé dish.

Bake until the top is lightly browned in patches, the edges are browned (this makes a nice crisp contrast to the soft interior), and the center looks set if you give the baking dish a slight jiggle, about 1 hour. It is okay to bake it for an additional 5 minutes if you are not sure if it is done.

Serve immediately. Use a large spoon to scoop out portions and pass butter to melt on top.

CHAPTER 03
REFRIGERATOR
BREADS

REFRIGERATOR BREADS

I'm as eager as anyone to bake bread that fits into my schedule and doesn't take up a lot of time, and these breads do exactly that. A refrigerator dough divides bread making into manageable steps and puts the baker in control. You mix the dough, put it into a bowl, and stash the bowl in the refrigerator. Then you shape, rise, and bake rolls, sweet buns, and crusty loaves when you want to eat them.

Every dough in this chapter rests in the refrigerator until you are ready to bake all or part of it. I often mix a batch of dough after dinner (I wash the dishes while the mixer kneads the dough) and put it in the refrigerator. Even though I am an experienced baker, I am always surprised at how little time it takes to mix up a batch or two of dough.

A day or two later—or sometimes even longer—I bake as many rolls as I need for that day, use part of a sweet dough for twists laced with cinnamon sugar, or bake a loaf of dark rye and have sandwich bread and toast for several days. I take out as much dough as I need, and then either punch down the dough (press out the air) that will remain in the refrigerator, or I skip punching it down, cover it carefully, and return it to the refrigerator. It doesn't seem to matter if the air is pressed out or not. The cold environment of the refrigerator prevents the dough from rising too much. And because the doughs spend at least hours and sometimes days in the refrigerator, I use active dry yeast, rather than instant yeast, for all but the dark rye.

Two sweet dough recipes are included in this chapter. For these, the yeast is dissolved in lukewarm milk and then mixed with the other ingredients, rather than mixed with the dry ingredients, my usual method. I find this technique works well for a dough with a large proportion of sugar, eggs, and butter to flour, because a sweet dough interacts differently with yeast than the usual bread dough.

The two artisanal breads in this chapter, Crusty Artisanal Bread (facing page) and Multigrain Crusty Bread (page 52), are long recipes, but making them requires a series of truly simple steps. You mix the dry ingredients with most of the water and beat to combine, let the dough rest, add the remaining water, and knead. Then you transfer the dough to a bowl and refrigerate for up to two days. Finally, you remove the dough from the refrigerator, shape it into long loaves or rounds, let them rise, transfer them to a baking sheet, slash, let rise again for a short time, and bake. Admittedly, that adds up to a lot of steps, but no step takes very long, which means that each bread will fit easily into your busy schedule.

CRUSTY ARTISANAL BREAD

INGREDIENTS

> 3 cups unbleached all-purpose flour

> 1 cup unbleached bread flour

> ¼ cup whole-wheat flour

> 1 tbsp kosher salt

> 2¼ tsp active dry yeast
  (one ¼-oz packet)

> 2 cups water, at room temperature

Before I began writing this book, I took a weeklong course taught by Richard Rice at his North Head Bakery on Grand Manan Island in Canada. All the students carted their stand mixers to the island and used them to make the dough for breads in all shapes and sizes. In addition to learning how to make about thirty different kinds of bread, I picked up a lot of basic knowledge from the course, some of which I want to pass along here.

First, a good artisanal loaf (small-batch handmade bread) requires only flour, salt, yeast, and water, and takes little active time to make; the final dough should be a soft mass that is just past the stick-to-the-bowl stage. A dough hook is best for kneading, but you can also knead by hand. Adding the correct amount of water is essential for achieving the ideal soft dough—a dough that jiggles like a bowl of gelatin and bakes up into a moist, crusty loaf. If you use too little water, the bread will be dry inside. If you use too much water, the bread will spread out, rather than rise, in the oven. We used nonchlorinated water from Richard's well, which guaranteed a better flavor and can be duplicated with filtered or spring water. A well-floured work surface is key to shaping the soft dough, and a long, slow rising, accomplished with refrigeration, is important to good flavor and texture.

If you are using a double baguette pan to bake two long loaves, form the dough into thin, even loaves, not *bâtards* with a thicker center. Thick centers will rise into each other and prevent crusting where they touch. I prefer to bake both long and round loaves on a baking sheet. The absence of pan sides means that a good crust forms on all sides of the bread.

CRUSTY
ARTISANAL BREAD

YIELD
Makes 2 round or long loaves,
or 1 of each

MIXING TIME
15 minutes

RESTING TIME
15 minutes

REFRIGERATOR TIME
Overnight or up to 2 days

RISING TIME
1 hour after refrigeration

BAKING
475°F for about 25 minutes

continued ↘

METHOD In a stand mixer fitted with the flat beater, mix together the 3 flours, the salt, and the yeast on low speed just until combined. Add 1¾ cups of the water and mix until all the ingredients are smoothly combined, then beat for 4 minutes. The dough will be soft and sticky and will not come away from the sides of the bowl. Cover the bowl with a clean kitchen towel and let the dough rest for 15 minutes. The flour will absorb some of the water and the dough will be less sticky.

Fit the mixer with the dough hook, add the remaining ¼ cup water, and beat on low speed for 6 minutes. After about 4 minutes, the still-soft dough should begin to come away from the sides of the bowl. If it does not, sprinkle in flour, 1 tsp at a time, adding just enough to allow the dough to come away from the sides of the bowl. On a dry winter day, additional flour will probably not be necessary. On a humid day, a small quantity of flour may be needed. The dough should be soft and very pliable.

To knead the dough by hand (see page 16), transfer it to a floured work surface and knead for about 5 minutes, adding just enough flour to keep the dough from sticking to the work surface.

Sprinkle a large, clean bowl with flour and transfer the dough to the bowl. Sprinkle the top lightly with flour. Cover the bowl with plastic wrap and refrigerate overnight or up to 2 days.

Remove the dough from the refrigerator and punch down the dough to press out the air. Divide the dough in half. For a round loaf, or *boule*, line a round 8-in basket or bowl with a clean kitchen towel. Dust the liner generously with flour. To form the *boule*, on a floured work surface, press half of the dough into an 8-in circle. Bring up four opposite edges to the center of the circle, and press firmly with a finger to seal them together. Then bring up the remaining four opposite edges of the circle—like gathering the edges of a piece of cloth into a sack—so that all of the edges are at the center, and press with a finger to seal. Carefully place the *boule*, seam-side up, in the lined basket. If making two *boules*, repeat with the remaining dough half and another basket. Sprinkle the top surface of each loaf lightly with flour, cover each with a clean kitchen towel, and let the dough rise for 45 minutes. The dough will look puffy and soft, but it will not rise a lot.

To form one or two baguettes or long loaves, place a heavy cloth (canvas is good) or clean kitchen towel on a rimless baking sheet and flour it, or flour one or two single or one double baguette pan. (The baking sheet makes it easy to move the risen bread and cloth.) On a floured work surface, pat half of the dough into a 6-by-4-in rectangle. Fold the rect-angle in half lengthwise and press the seam to seal. Use your palms to roll the dough back and forth, gently moving your palms along the length of the dough to make a loaf as long as you want. I recommend you make it about 9 in long. To taper the ends and leave the middle thicker for a *bâtard*, increase the pressure as you move toward the ends. Place the loaf, seam-side up, on the floured cloth, and roll up the cloth against the long sides of the loaf to support it as it rises. Or, put the loaf, seam-side down, in the floured baguette pan. If making two long loaves, repeat with the remaining dough half and another baking sheet and cloth or the remaining baguette furrow. Sprinkle the top of each loaf lightly with flour, cover with a clean kitchen towel, and let the dough rise for 45 minutes. The dough will look puffy and soft, but it will not rise a lot.

When the dough has risen for 35 minutes, position a rack in the middle of the oven and preheat to 475°F. Have ready a metal pie pan with a clean rock in it or an empty metal pie pan. If not using a baguette pan, sprinkle a baking sheet with flour.

When the dough has risen for 45 minutes, gently tip the dough in one of the baskets onto the pan, or unroll both ends of the cloth and lift one end to roll the long loaf onto the pan. Repeat with the second loaf. The loaves should now be seam-side down and at least 2 in apart. Slide them gently to separate them, if necessary. Using a small, sharp knife, and holding it at roughly a 45-degree angle to the top of the bread, cut a long slash or a crisscross in the top of the round loaves, or a series of four or five evenly spaced, diagonal slashes along the width of the baguettes. Cut firmly to make each slash about ¼ in deep. Sprinkle flour lightly on top of each loaf and re-cover with the kitchen towel. Let rise for 15 minutes.

Put the metal pie pan on the lowest rack in the oven 5 min-utes before the bread is ready to go into the oven. When the bread is ready, sprinkle about 2 tbsp water over the rock to create steam, or sprinkle the same amount into the empty pan. There should be a burst of steam at the beginning and the steam should last for about the first one-third of the baking time. Put the bread in the oven and bake until browned and crusty, about 25 minutes. The bread will rise 1½ to 2 in during baking. Remove from the oven, immediately slide onto wire racks, and let cool completely.

You may hear crackling sounds as the bread cools, which is good. The cooled bread will have a firm, but not hard crust. The interior will be moist with holes that vary from tiny to about ¼ in in diameter. Use a serrated knife to slice the bread.

The bread can be stored in a paper bag at room temperature for up to 3 days. If the bread is cut, wrap a piece of plastic wrap around the cut end before slipping it into the bag. To serve, preheat the oven to 275°F and heat the loaf, placed directly on the oven rack, until the crust is crisp and feels warm, about 10 minutes.

MULTIGRAIN CRUSTY BREAD

INGREDIENTS

Dough
> 3 cups unbleached all-purpose flour
> 1 cup unbleached bread flour
> ½ cup whole-wheat flour
> ¼ cup toasted sunflower seeds
> 2 tbsp steel-cut oats
> 2 tbsp medium-grind stone-ground yellow cornmeal
> 1 tbsp toasted sesame seeds
> 1 tbsp wheat bran
> 1 tbsp oat bran
> 1 tbsp kosher salt
> 2¼ tsp active dry yeast (one ¼-oz packet)
> 2¼ cups water, at room temperature

Moist, loaded with seeds and grains, and with a crisp crust, this is an appealing bread. Form the dough into two baguettes or rounds, or one of each. The seed and grain additions can be adjusted as desired, adding more of what you like and omitting what you don't like. Just keep in mind that the total amount of seeds and grains should remain the same. See Grain Gains (page 11) for information on the various grains used here. If you buy raw, rather than toasted, sunflower and sesame seeds, you can easily toast them in an oven preheated to 325°F for about 5 minutes, or until you can smell the seeds, they have taken on color, and they look shiny from their oil rising to the surface.

This recipe uses the same method as Crusty Artisanal Bread (page 49). Read the introduction to that recipe for tips on making and shaping the dough and on what equipment you will need. During the final mixing and addition of water, the dough should be soft and sticky but pull away from the sides of the bowl about halfway through the mixing.

METHOD Make the dough. In a stand mixer fitted with the flat beater, mix together the 3 flours, the sunflower seeds, oats, cornmeal, sesame seeds, wheat bran, oat bran, salt, and yeast on low speed just until combined. Add 2 cups of the water and mix until all the ingredients are smoothly combined; then beat for 4 minutes. The dough will be soft and sticky and will not come away from the sides of the bowl. Cover the bowl with a clean kitchen towel and let the dough rest for 15 minutes. The flour will absorb some of the water, and the dough will be less sticky.

continued ↘

MULTIGRAIN CRUSTY BREAD

Topping

> 1 tbsp raw sunflower seeds

> 1 tbsp steel-cut oats

> 1 tbsp medium-grind stone-ground yellow cornmeal

> 1 tbsp toasted sesame seeds

> 1 tbsp oat bran

YIELD
Makes 2 round or long loaves, or 1 of each

MIXING TIME
15 minutes

RESTING TIME
15 minutes

REFRIGERATOR TIME
Overnight or up to 2 days

RISING TIME
1 hour after refrigeration

BAKING
475°F for about 25 minutes

continued ↘

Fit the mixer with the dough hook, add the remaining ¼ cup water, and beat on low speed for 6 minutes. After about 4 minutes, the still-soft dough should begin to come away from the sides of the bowl. If it does not, sprinkle in flour, 1 tsp at a time, adding just enough to allow the dough to come away from the sides of the bowl. On a dry winter day, additional flour will probably not be necessary. On a humid day, a small quantity of flour may be needed. The dough should be soft and very pliable.

To knead the dough by hand (see page 16), place it on a floured work surface and knead for about 5 minutes, adding just enough flour to keep the dough from sticking to the work surface.

Sprinkle a clean large bowl with flour and transfer the dough to the bowl. Sprinkle the top lightly with flour. Cover the bowl with plastic wrap and refrigerate overnight or up to 2 days.

Remove the dough from the refrigerator and punch down the dough to press out the air. Divide the dough in half. For a round loaf or *boule*, line a round 8-in basket or bowl with a clean kitchen towel. Dust the liner generously with flour. To form the *boule*, on a floured work surface, press half of the dough into an 8-in circle. Bring up four opposite edges to the center of the circle, and press firmly with a finger to seal them together. Then bring up the remaining four opposite edges of the circle—like gathering the edges of a piece of cloth into a sack—so that all of the edges are at the center, and press with a finger to seal. Carefully place the *boule*, seam-side up, in the lined basket. If making two *boules*, repeat with the remaining dough half and another basket. Sprinkle the top of each loaf lightly with flour, cover each with a clean kitchen towel, and let the dough rise for 45 minutes. The dough will look puffy and soft, but it will not rise a lot.

To form one or two baguettes or long loaves, place a heavy cloth (canvas is good) or clean kitchen towel on a rimless baking sheet and flour it, or flour one or two single baguette pans or one double. (The baking sheet makes it easy to move the risen bread and cloth.) On a floured work surface, pat half of the dough into a 6-by-4-in rectangle. Fold the rectangle in half lengthwise and press the seam to seal. Use your palms to roll the dough back and forth, gently moving your palms along the length of the dough to make a loaf as long as you want. I recommend you make it about 9 in long. To taper the ends and leave the middle thicker for a *bâtard*, increase the pressure as you move toward the ends. Place the loaf, seam-side up, on the floured cloth, and roll up the cloth against the long sides of the loaf to support it as it rises. Or, put the loaf, seam-side down, in the floured baguette pan. If making two long loaves, repeat with the remaining dough half and another baking sheet and cloth or the remaining baguette furrow. Sprinkle the top of each loaf lightly with flour, cover with a clean kitchen towel, and let the dough rise for 45 minutes. The dough will look puffy and soft, but it will not rise a lot.

When the dough has risen for 35 minutes, position a rack in the middle of the oven and preheat to 475°F. Have ready a metal pie pan with a clean rock in it or an empty metal pie pan. If not using a baguette pan, sprinkle a baking sheet with cornmeal.

When the dough has risen for 45 minutes, gently tip the dough in one of the baskets onto the pan, or unroll both ends of the cloth and lift one end to roll the long loaf onto the prepared pan. Repeat with the second loaf. The loaves should now be seam-side down and at least 2 in apart. Slide them gently to separate them, if necessary.

Make the topping. In a small bowl, stir together the sunflower seeds, steel-cut oats, cornmeal, sesame seeds, and oat bran. Use a pastry brush to brush water lightly over the top of each loaf. Sprinkle the topping over each, dividing it evenly and pressing it gently into the dough. Using a small, sharp knife, and holding it at a roughly 45-degree angle to the top of the bread, cut a long slash in the top of the round loaves, or a series of three evenly spaced, diagonal slashes along the width of the baguettes. Cut firmly to make each slash about ¼ in deep. Sprinkle flour lightly on top of each loaf and re-cover with the kitchen towel. Let rise for 15 minutes.

Put the metal pie pan on the lower rack of the oven 5 minutes before the bread is ready to go into the oven. When the bread is ready, sprinkle about 2 tbsp water over the rock to create steam, or sprinkle the same amount into the empty pan. There should only be a burst of steam at the beginning and the steam should last for about the first one-third of the baking time. Put the bread in the oven and bake until browned and crusty, about 25 minutes. The bread will rise 1½ to 2 in during baking. Remove from the oven, immediately slide onto wire racks, and let cool completely.

You may hear crackling as the bread cools, which is good. The cooled bread will have a crisp crust. The interior will be moist with holes that vary from tiny to about ¼ in. Use a serrated knife to slice the bread.

The bread can be stored in a paper bag at room temperature for up to 3 days. If the bread is cut, wrap a piece of plastic wrap around the cut end before slipping it into the bag. To serve, preheat the oven to 275°F and heat the uncut loaf, placed directly on the oven rack, until the crust is crisp and feels warm, about 10 minutes. This is also a good bread to slice and toast.

BRIOCHE

INGREDIENTS

> ¼ cup milk, any fat content

> 2¼ tsp active dry yeast
  (one ¼-oz packet)

> 1 tbsp sugar

> 4 large eggs, at room temperature

> 2½ cups unbleached all-purpose flour

> 1 tsp kosher salt

> 1¼ cups unsalted butter, at room
  temperature, cut into 1-inch pieces

> 1 large egg, lightly beaten, for glaze

YIELD
Makes 2 large or 10 individual breads

MIXING TIME
15 minutes

REFRIGERATOR TIME
Overnight or up to 2 days

RISING TIME
1 to 2 hours after refrigeration

BAKING
375°F for about 45 minutes for large,
about 35 minutes for individual

Brioche gets its lavish quality from butter and eggs. Both ingredients help to produce the golden color, eggs contribute to the light texture, and butter—lots of it—ensures the crisp, buttery crust that surrounds the best loaves. You can buy fluted brioche molds in many sizes for baking this dough, or you can use loaf pans.

METHOD In a small saucepan, heat the milk over low heat to about 110°F on an instant-read thermometer. Remove from the heat and pour into the large bowl of a stand mixer fitted with the flat beater. Stir in the yeast and sugar and let sit until the yeast is foamy, about 5 minutes.

On low speed, mix in the eggs, two at a time, incorporating each addition before adding the next one. Add the flour and salt and continue mixing until the flour is incorporated. Add the butter, several pieces at a time, again incorporating each addition before adding the next one. Continue mixing on low speed until the dough looks smooth, 8 to 10 minutes. It will look like a thick cake batter. As you mix, stop and scrape down the bowl sides and beater as necessary.

Using a plastic dough scraper, scrape the dough into a buttered bowl. Cover the bowl with plastic wrap and refrigerate overnight or up to 2 days. The dough will almost double in size.

Butter two 4-cup brioche pans, two 8½-by-4½-by-2½-in loaf pans, one 9-by-5-by-3-in loaf pan, ten individual brioche molds each with a 6-tbsp capacity, or a combination of pans. Remove the dough from the refrigerator and punch it down to press out the air.

If you are using two large brioche pans, remove two walnut-sized pieces of the dough, shape into two small, smooth balls with your hands, and set aside. Divide the remaining dough in half. Use your hands to form half of the dough into a large, smooth ball. Place the ball into a prepared pan. Repeat with the second half of the dough and place in the second pan.

Press an indentation into the center of each ball, and put a small dough ball (the topknot) into each indentation.

If you are using two loaf pans, divide the dough into quarters. Use your hands to roll each quarter into a 4-by-2-in oval. Place two ovals in each prepared pan, placing them end to end so they just touch each other. They will almost fill the bottom of the pan. If you are using the single larger loaf pan, divide the dough into quarters. Use your hands to roll each quarter into a large oval that will come about two-thirds of the way up the sides of the pan. Place the ovals side by side and end to end in the pan so they just touch one another. A long side of each oval will touch the long sides of the pan.

If you are using individual brioche pans, place the pans on a baking sheet. Divide the dough into 10 equal pieces, and shape each piece into a smooth ball with your hands. Place a ball in each pan.

Cover with plastic wrap and let rise in a draft-free spot for 1 to 2 hours. The timing will depend on the temperature of your kitchen—the colder the kitchen, the longer it takes for all of the cold butter in the dough to soften. The dough will come to room temperature, will look puffed, and will nearly double in size. It should almost fill the pans. When the dough has about 20 minutes of rising time remaining, position a rack in the middle of the oven and preheat to 375°F.

Lightly brush the top of the dough with the beaten egg. Bake the brioches until they are browned on top, fill the pans, and rise about 1 in above the rims, about 45 minutes for the larger pans and 35 minutes for the individual pans. A toothpick inserted in the center of the bread will come out clean. Let cool in the pans on wire racks for 10 minutes. Turn out onto the racks and let cool completely. Slice and serve the large loaves or serve the individual brioches whole.

The brioches can be stored in a plastic bag at room temperature for up to 3 days.

DARK RYE BREAD

INGREDIENTS

> 2 cups unbleached all-purpose flour

> 1 tbsp unsweetened Dutch-process cocoa powder

> 1½ tsp kosher salt

> 2¼ tsp instant yeast (one ¼-oz packet)

> 1 cup hot water (about 130°F)

> 2 tbsp unsulfured light molasses

> 1 cup medium rye flour

> 1 tbsp plus 1 tsp caraway seeds

> Corn or canola oil and stone-ground yellow cornmeal for pan

Here is a good combination that is not always easy to produce: a close-grained, moist bread with a light texture and robust flavor. The way to achieve a good rye dough (or any bread dough) that is not too heavy is to include enough liquid. Rye flour is low in gluten, which means the dough doesn't rise much. Adding some all-purpose flour allows the dough to stretch and rise, to lighten both the texture and flavor. Also, even though this is a refrigerator bread, I use instant yeast, because it gives a boost to the rising. This loaf slices cleanly and neatly with a serrated knife, making it a good sandwich bread.

METHOD In a stand mixer fitted with the flat beater, beat together 1 cup of the all-purpose flour, the cocoa powder, salt, and yeast on low speed just until combined. Add the hot water and mix until all the ingredients are smoothly combined, then beat for 2 minutes. Add the molasses, the remaining 1 cup all-purpose flour, and the rye flour. Continue mixing on low speed for 5 minutes, adding the caraway seeds after 4 minutes. Stop to scrape down the bowl sides and beater as necessary. The dough will be soft but will come away from the sides of the bowl. The dough is ready if when you stop the mixer and stick your finger into the dough, your finger comes out clean.

Transfer the dough to an oiled bowl, and then turn the dough to coat it with oil on both sides. Cover the bowl with plastic wrap and refrigerate overnight. The dough will increase in size by about half but will not double.

Oil about one-third of a baking sheet or about half of a pizza pan and sprinkle the oiled surface generously with cornmeal. You only need to oil the part of the pan on which the bread will sit.

Remove the dough from the refrigerator, remove the dough from the bowl, and punch it down to press out the air. On a lightly floured surface, pat the dough into a flat oval about 9 in long. Starting from a long side, roll up the oval. The loaf will be about 9 in long and narrower at the ends than in the center. The dough is elastic, making it easy to shape. Place the dough roll on the oiled part of the pan.

Cover the bread lightly with plastic wrap and let rise for 1 hour. The loaf will rise only slightly. When the dough has risen for 40 minutes, position a rack in the middle of the oven and preheat to 350°F. When the dough has risen for 50 minutes, put a clean rock on a metal pie pan and put the pan on the lowest rack of the oven (or, lacking a rock, put the empty pan on the rack).

When the bread is ready to go into the oven, pour about 2 tbsp water over the rock in the pie pan to create steam (or directly into the empty pan). Put the bread in the oven and bake until the top is firm and crusty and the bottom is browned, about 35 minutes. The bread will rise about 1 in during baking. Remove from the oven and immediately slide the loaf onto a wire rack to cool completely. The crust on top will be firm but not exceptionally crisp when cooled.

The bread can be baked up to 2 days ahead and stored in a plastic bag at room temperature. Once it is cut, continue to store it in a plastic bag to keep it fresh.

YIELD
Makes 1 oval loaf

MIXING TIME
10 minutes

REFRIGERATOR TIME
Overnight

RISING TIME
1 hour after refrigeration

BAKING
350°F for about 35 minutes

PARKER HOUSE ROLLS

INGREDIENTS

> ½ cup whole milk

> 2 tbsp unsalted butter

> 3¾ cups unbleached all-purpose flour

> ½ cup granulated sugar

> 1 tsp kosher salt

> 4½ tsp active dry yeast (two ¼-oz packets)

> 2 large eggs

> 1 cup sour cream

> 5½ tbsp unsalted butter, 3½ tbsp at room temperature, for filling rolls; 2 tbsp unsalted butter, melted, for brushing rolls

Parker House rolls originated at the Parker House Hotel (founded by Harvey Parker) in Boston in the 1870s. The venerable hotel is now the Omni Parker House, and the soft, subtly sweet, buttery rolls are still served there. They are formed by folding a round of dough over on itself. Once baked, the fold opens easily and the roll is ready to be slathered with butter or jam, or both.

The refrigerated dough is easy to shape and the rolls rise in only about thirty minutes, before they are popped into the oven, where they quickly become hot, homemade dinner rolls. I have also included instructions on how to form cloverleaf rolls (see Choices).

METHOD In a small saucepan, heat the milk and butter over medium heat to about 130°F on an instant-read thermometer. Remove from the heat.

In a stand mixer fitted with the flat beater, mix together 1 cup of the flour, the sugar, salt, and yeast on low speed just until combined. Add the hot milk mixture and mix until all the ingredients are smoothly combined, then beat for 2 minutes. With the mixer still on low speed, add the eggs and sour cream and beat until blended. Add the remaining 2¾ cups flour and continue mixing for 5 minutes. Stop to scrape down the bowl sides and beater as necessary. The dough will be very soft but should come away from the sides of the bowl.

Transfer the dough to a large buttered bowl, and then turn the dough to coat it with butter on both sides. Cover the bowl with plastic wrap and refrigerate over-night or up to 2 days. The dough will about double in size.

Line a baking sheet with parchment paper. Remove the dough from the refrigera-tor, and divide it in half. On a floured work surface, pat half of the dough into a thick circle, then roll out into an 11-in circle ½ in thick. Rolling out the dough will press out the air, so you don't need to punch it down. Using a 2½-in round biscuit cutter, and dipping it in flour before each use, cut out circles. Using the dull edge of a table knife, make a crease in the center or slightly off center on each circle. Spread about ½ tsp of the room-temperature butter on the crease of a circle and fold the dough over itself along the crease. Press at the edges of the fold to seal the ends of the roll and gently press to seal the edge along the top of the roll. After *many* experiments, I have found that this technique holds the folded top in place and at the same time allows it to pull away slightly during baking. Repeat with the remaining circles. Place the rolls on the prepared baking sheet ½ in apart if you want the rolls to touch one another and form soft edges during baking, or 1 in apart if you want the rolls to remain separated and brown slightly on the edges. Repeat with the second half of the dough. Then gather the dough scraps and roll and cut to make more rolls. Brush the tops of the rolls with 1 tbsp of the melted butter.

Cover the rolls lightly with plastic wrap and let rise until slightly puffed, about 30 minutes. The dough will not rise much. Most of the rising happens during baking. When the rolls have risen for 10 minutes, position a rack in the middle of the oven and preheat to 350°F.

Bake until the tops are just beginning to brown and the bottoms are browned, about 22 minutes. Use a spatula to slide the rolls onto a wire rack, then brush with the remaining 1 tbsp melted butter. Serve warm or at room temperature.

The rolls can be baked up to 2 days ahead, covered, and stored at room temperature. To serve, preheat the oven to 250°F and reheat the rolls, covered, until warm, about 15 minutes.

CHOICES To make cloverleaf rolls, roll pieces of dough into 1¼-in balls. Using standard muffin tins, butter 16 wells. Place three dough balls in each prepared well. Brush with melted butter, cover, let rise, and bake as directed.

YIELD
Makes 18 to 20 rolls

MIXING TIME
10 minutes

REFRIGERATOR TIME
Overnight or up to 2 days

RISING TIME
About 30 minutes after refrigeration

BAKING
350°F for about 22 minutes

ANYTIME BUTTER TWISTS

INGREDIENTS

> ¾ cup whole milk

> 2½ cups unbleached all-purpose flour

> 2 tbsp granulated sugar

> ½ tsp kosher salt

> 2¼ tsp active dry yeast
  (one ¼-oz packet)

> 1 large egg

> ½ cup cold unsalted butter, cut
  into about 16 pieces, plus 5 tbsp melted,
  for brushing twists

Versatile is the word for this bread. The soft dough must chill in the refrigerator for at least four hours, but it can remain there for up to four days, ready to form into bread whenever you like. The dough makes eight twists, but you can bake four twists at a time. The easiest and best way to mix this dough is by hand.

Numerous seasonings can be added to the twists when they are formed. Coarse sea salt or kosher salt and freshly ground black pepper, ¼ cup grated Parmesan cheese, ¼ cup finely chopped onion, or 1 tbsp finely chopped garlic can be sprinkled over the rolled dough. Or, 2 tsp sesame seeds, caraway seeds, poppy seeds, or dried herbs are other possibilities.

METHOD In a small saucepan, heat the milk over medium heat to about 130°F on an instant-read thermometer.

In a large bowl, and using a large spoon, stir together 1 cup of the flour, the sugar, salt, and yeast. Add the hot milk and stir to combine. Stir in the egg until blended.

Put the remaining 1½ cups flour in a medium bowl and scatter the cold butter pieces over the top. Using your thumb and fingertips, two table knives, or a pastry blender, work the butter into the flour until flour-coated pea-sized pieces form. Stir the butter-flour mixture into the milk mixture until the flour is moistened and a sticky dough forms. You will see pieces of butter; this is good. Cover the bowl with plastic wrap and refrigerate for 4 hours or up to 4 days. The dough will about double in size. Once the soft dough is cold, it is easy to roll and twist.

If you are baking half of the dough or less, line a baking sheet with parchment paper. If you are baking all of the dough, prepare two baking sheets. Remove half of the dough from the refrigerator. On a lightly floured work surface, roll out the dough into a rectangle 10 by 4 in and about ⅜ in thick.

Rolling out the dough will press out the air, so you don't need to punch it down. If necessary, pat the dough to make the edges of the rectangle even. Brush with about 1 tbsp of the melted butter. If desired, sprinkle with one of the seasonings suggested in the introductory note, pressing them lightly onto the dough.

Using a sharp knife, cut the dough into four strips, each 1 in wide and 10 in long. Pick up one strip, holding each end with one hand. Twist the ends in opposite directions to create a tightly twisted strip. The dough will stretch about 1 in as you twist it to make a twist 11 in long. Place the twist on a prepared baking sheet. Repeat with the three remaining strips and add to the baking sheet, spacing them 2 in apart. Brush the twists lightly with some of the melted butter. Roll out and shape the remaining half of the dough the same way, place on the second prepared sheet, and brush with the remaining butter. Or, cover the remaining dough with plastic wrap, pressing the wrap directly onto the surface, and leave it in the refrigerator to shape another day, keeping in mind you must use it within 4 days of when it was first refrigerated.

Cover the buttered twists lightly with plastic wrap and let rise until slightly puffed, about 30 minutes. The dough will not rise much. Most of the rising happens during baking. When the dough has risen for 10 minutes, position a rack in the middle of the oven and preheat to 375°F.

Bake the twists one sheet at a time until the tops are lightly browned and the bottoms are browned, about 20 minutes. Let cool on the pan on a wire rack for 15 minutes. Serve warm.

The twists can be baked up to 2 days ahead, covered, and stored at room temperature. To serve, preheat the oven to 250°F and reheat the twists until warm, about 15 minutes.

YIELD
Makes 8 twists

MIXING TIME
10 minutes

REFRIGERATOR TIME
4 hours or up to 4 days

RISING TIME
About 30 minutes after refrigeration

BAKING
375°F for about 20 minutes

CINNAMON TWISTS

When I was growing up in Lakeland, Florida, we would go to Maas Brothers department store in the "big city" of Tampa for an occasional shopping spree. For me, the highlight of the day was lunch in the store's restaurant, where baskets of cinnamon twists were served. These sweet rolls, with cinnamon sugar swirling through their soft centers and forming a crisp glaze on top, are reminiscent of those childhood treats.

METHOD Make the dough and refrigerate as directed.

Butter a 9-in square or 11-by-7-in pan.

On a lightly floured work surface, roll out the dough into a 12-in square. Rolling out the dough will press out the air, so you don't need to punch it down. Brush the dough with 1 tbsp of the melted butter. Sprinkle ¼ cup of the cinnamon sugar over the dough, leaving a ½-in border uncovered on all sides. Fold one-third of the dough over onto the square. Brush the folded portion lightly with some of the remaining melted butter, and then sprinkle the remaining cinnamon sugar over the buttered surface. Now, fold the two dough layers over to meet the bottom edge of the original dough square and press to seal all the edges. You will have a three-layered strip that measures 12 in long and about 4 in wide.

Cut the dough strip crosswise into twelve equal pieces each about 1 in wide. Pick up one strip, holding each end with one hand. Twist the ends in opposite directions to create a tightly twisted strip. Repeat to make five more twists and then place the six twists in a row along the top half of the prepared pan; they will just touch. Repeat with the remaining strips and place in a row along the bottom half of the pan. Brush the tops of the twists lightly with the remaining melted butter and sprinkle over the tops any cinnamon sugar that fell out of the twists during shaping and transferring. Some of the sugar will fall onto the bottom of the pan and will form a light glaze during baking.

INGREDIENTS

> ½ recipe (21 oz) Sweet Dough for Extra-Sticky Caramel-Pecan Buns (page 71)

> 2 tbsp unsalted butter, melted

> ½ cup granulated sugar mixed with 1 tsp ground cinnamon

YIELD
Makes 12 twists

MIXING TIME
15 minutes for dough and filling

REFRIGERATOR TIME
Overnight or up to 3 days

RISING TIME
About 40 minutes after refrigeration

BAKING
375°F for about 40 minutes

Cover the twists lightly with plastic wrap and let rise until puffy, about 40 minutes. The dough will not double in size. When the twists have risen for 20 minutes, position a rack in the middle of the oven and preheat to 375°F.

Bake the twists until the edges and tops are browned, about 40 minutes. They will spread into a single, large pull-apart cake as they bake. Let cool on the pan on a wire rack for 5 minutes. Use a small, sharp knife to loosen the twists from the sides of the pan. Invert a wire rack on top of the pan, and holding the rack and pan firmly together with pot holders, invert them together. Carefully lift off the pan. Invert a second wire rack on top of the twists, invert the racks together, and lift off the top rack. The twists are now right-side up. Let cool for at least 15 minutes before serving. To serve, cut or pull apart.

The twists can be covered and stored at room temperature overnight. To serve, preheat the oven to oven to 250°F and reheat the twists, covered, until warm, about 15 minutes.

A CHOCOLATE-HAZELNUT BABKA & A CINNAMON BABKA

INGREDIENTS

Dough
> ½ cup whole milk
> 4½ tsp active dry yeast
  (two ¼-oz packets)
> 3 cups unbleached all-purpose flour
> ½ cup granulated sugar
> 1 tsp kosher salt
> 1 tsp grated lemon zest
> 2 large eggs
> 2 large egg yolks
> 1 tsp pure vanilla extract
> ½ cup unsalted butter, melted

Even though Jerry Seinfeld lost out on the chocolate *babka* and had to settle for the cinnamon *babka*, you can have both. This recipe makes enough dough for two of these rich yeasted coffee cakes that originated in the Jewish kitchens of eastern Europe. (The term *babka* is also used for a coffee cake of western Russian and Polish origin, traditionally with a fruit filling.) If you want to use the same filling for both loaves, double the ingredients for the filling. The cake's many layers are formed by shaping the filled dough into a long roll, curving the roll into a figure eight and then twisting it before putting it into the pan.

METHOD Make the dough. In a small saucepan, heat the milk over medium heat to about 110°F on an instant-read thermometer. Remove from the heat and pour into the large bowl of a stand mixer fitted with the flat beater. Stir in the yeast and let sit until foamy, about 5 minutes.

Add 1 cup of the flour, the sugar, salt, and lemon zest to the yeast mixture and beat on low speed until smooth, about 2 minutes. Beat in the eggs, egg yolks, and vanilla until combined. Add the remaining 2 cups flour and beat for 1 minute. Add the melted butter in three additions, letting the butter blend into the dough before adding the next addition. Then continue to beat on low speed for 6 minutes. The dough is ready when it is soft and sticky, pulls away from the sides of the bowl, and if you stop the mixer and stick a finger into the dough, your finger comes out clean.

Transfer the dough to a large buttered bowl and then turn the dough to coat it with butter on both sides. Cover the bowl with plastic wrap and refrigerate overnight or up to 2 days. The dough will about double in size.

continued ↘

A CHOCOLATE-HAZELNUT BABKA & A CINNAMON BABKA

Chocolate-Hazelnut Filling

> ¾ cup toasted, peeled, and chopped hazelnuts

> ½ cup granulated sugar

> 1 large egg white

> 1 tsp pure vanilla extract

> 3 tbsp unsalted butter, at room temperature

> 4 oz bittersweet chocolate, coarsely chopped

Cinnamon Filling

> ½ cup granulated sugar

> ½ cup packed light brown sugar

> 1½ tsp ground cinnamon

> ¼ cup unsalted butter, at room temperature, plus 2 tbsp melted, for brushing dough.

continued ↘

Make the chocolate-hazelnut filling. In a food processor, combine the hazelnuts and sugar and process until the nuts are finely ground, about 15 seconds. Add the egg white and vanilla and process until blended, about 5 seconds. With the processor running, add the room-temperature butter and process until the mixture forms a ball, about 40 seconds. Reserve the chocolate.

Make the cinnamon filling. In a medium bowl, stir together the granulated sugar, brown sugar, and cinnamon. Reserve the butter.

Make the crumbs. In a medium bowl, stir together the flour, brown sugar, and salt. Scatter the butter pieces over the top. Using your thumb and finger tips, two table knives, or a pastry blender, work the butter into the flour mixture until crumbs form. You will have about 4 cups. Put half of the crumbs in a small bowl.

Form the coffee cakes. Butter two 9-by-5-by-3-in loaf pans.

Remove the dough from the refrigerator and divide it in half. On a floured work surface, roll out half of the dough into a 13-by-8-in rectangle. Rolling out the dough will press out the air, so you don't need to punch it down. Brush the dough with 1 tbsp of the melted butter. For the chocolate-hazelnut cake, use a metal spatula to spread the filling evenly over the dough, leaving a ½-in border uncovered on all sides. Sprinkle the reserved chocolate evenly over the filling, again leaving the border uncovered. Starting at the long side, roll up the dough tightly into a roll. Pinch all of the edges to seal them. Brush the roll with 1 tbsp of the melted butter. Form the roll into a figure eight, pressing the ends together to seal them. Do not worry if the figure eight is not perfectly even. Holding each end of the figure eight in one hand, twist the ends in opposite directions once and then put the figure eight into a prepared pan. Sprinkle the crumbs from the small bowl over the dough, letting them spill down the sides. Cover lightly with plastic wrap.

Use a thin spatula to spread the ¼ cup soft butter on the remaining dough and repeat to make a second twisted loaf using the cinnamon filling. Put the loaf in the second prepared pan, sprinkle with the crumbs in the medium bowl, and cover lightly with plastic wrap.

Let the cakes rise until slightly puffed, about 1 hour. The dough will not rise much. Most of the rising happens during baking. When the cakes have risen for 40 minutes, position a rack in the middle of the oven and preheat to 350°F.

Bake the cakes until the tops feel firm and are golden brown, about 45 minutes. They will rise to at least the tops of the pans. Let cool in the pans on wire racks for 30 minutes. Use a small, sharp knife to loosen the edges of each cake from its pan, then turn the cakes out onto the wire racks to cool completely. Dust with powdered sugar just before serving.

The coffee cakes can be stored in a plastic bag at room temperature for up to 3 days. They are also good sliced and toasted.

CHOICES Use half of the dough and one of the fillings and bake the second *babka* the next day. Substitute toasted or untoasted natural almonds for the hazelnuts. To give the chocolate-hazelnut *babka* an extra dose of chocolate, omit the powdered sugar and drizzle 2 oz bittersweet chocolate, melted, over the top of the baked and cooled *babka*.

Crumbs
> *1½ cups unbleached all-purpose flour*
> *1 cup packed light brown sugar*
> *1 tsp salt*
> *½ cup cold unsalted butter, cut into pieces*
> *Powdered sugar for dusting the top*

YIELD
Makes 2 coffee cakes

MIXING TIME
30 minutes for dough, filling, and crumbs

REFRIGERATOR TIME
Overnight or up to 2 days

RISING TIME
About 1 hour after refrigeration

BAKING
350°F for about 45 minutes

EXTRA-STICKY CARAMEL-PECAN BUNS

....

INGREDIENTS

Sweet Dough
> 1 cup whole milk
> 4½ tsp active dry yeast
  (two ¼-oz packets)
> ½ cup unsalted butter,
  at room temperature
> ½ cup granulated sugar
> 1 tsp kosher salt
> 2 large eggs
> 4¼ cups unbleached all-purpose flour

Caramel Glaze
> ½ cup unsalted butter
> ¼ cup honey
> 1½ cups packed light brown sugar
> ½ cup whole milk
> 1¾ cups pecan halves

I spent years experimenting with sweet doughs to find one that baked into a soft, light-textured dough for sticky buns and sweet rolls. I never did succeed. But when my husband took up bread baking, he brought my search to a happy ending. This golden dough has a buttery flavor but is not overly rich, and it bakes into a soft bun covered with crisp caramel-coated pecans. The result is a tender interior that contrasts perfectly with the crunchy nuts. I roll the dough out into a narrow rectangle and then roll it up into a slim cylinder, to yield small, spiraled buns with lots of cinnamon filling.

The recipe yields 2 lb 10 oz of dough, and one-fourth of the dough weighs 10½ oz. I also use this dough for making Cinnamon Buns with Cream Cheese Glaze (page 74) and Cinnamon Twists (page 64).

METHOD Make the dough. In a small saucepan, heat the milk over medium heat to about 110°F on an instant-read thermometer. Remove from the heat and stir the yeast into the milk. Let sit until the yeast is foamy, about 5 minutes.

In a stand mixer fitted with the flat beater, beat together the butter, sugar, and salt on low speed until blended, about 1 minute. Add the eggs and beat until creamy and smooth, about 2 minutes. With the mixer still on low speed, add 1 cup of the flour and beat until incorporated. Add the yeast mixture and beat until the mixture looks creamy and smooth, about 2 minutes. Then add the remaining 3¼ cups flour and beat for 2 minutes. The dough should be soft and sticky and will not pull away from the sides of the bowl. Stop the mixer and stick your finger in the dough. It is ready if your finger comes out clean.

continued ↘

EXTRA-STICKY
CARAMEL-PECAN BUNS

Filling
> 4 tbsp unsalted butter, at room temperature

> 1 cup packed light brown sugar mixed with 1½ tsp ground cinnamon

YIELD
Makes 56 small buns

MIXING TIME
20 minutes for dough, filling, and glaze

REFRIGERATOR TIME
Overnight or up to 2 days

RISING TIME
About 45 minutes after refrigeration

BAKING
350°F for about 25 minutes

continued ↘

Transfer the dough to a large buttered bowl, and then turn the dough to coat it with butter on both sides. Cover the bowl with plastic wrap and refrigerate overnight or up to 2 days. The dough will about double in size.

Make the glaze before you form the buns. Line the bottom of two 9-in square or round pans or two 11-by-7-in pans with parchment paper. The pans should have at least 2-in sides.

In a medium saucepan, combine the butter, honey, brown sugar, and milk over medium heat. Heat, stirring often, until the butter and sugar melt. Increase the heat to medium-high and bring to a rolling boil that cannot be stirred down. Remove from the heat and pour half of the glaze into each prepared pan. If using round pans, start at the edge of each pan and arrange the pecan halves, flat bottom–side up, in tight concentric circles in the bottom of the pan. If using square or rectangular pans, arrange the pecans in tight, neat rows. Let the glaze cool while you form the buns. (The glaze and nuts can be prepared in the pans a day ahead, covered, and refrigerated.)

Use a knife to mark the cold dough into quarters. Remove one-fourth of the dough (10½ oz) from the refrigerator. On a floured work surface, roll out the dough into a 14-by-7-in rectangle. Rolling out the dough will press the air out, so you don't need to punch it down.

Make the filling. Cut 1 tbsp of the room-temperature butter into small pieces, and drop the pieces evenly over the rectangle. Using a thin spatula and leaving a 1-in border uncovered on all sides, spread the butter thinly over the dough. There will be some blank spaces. Sprinkle one-fourth of the cinnamon sugar evenly over the buttered surface, leaving the border uncovered. Starting at a long side, roll up the dough tightly into a roll 14 in long. Pinch all of the edges to seal them, and then, if necessary, pull the dough gently to extend it to 14 in.

Using a large, sharp knife and a slight sawing motion, cut the roll crosswise into 14 equal pieces. Place the pieces, just touching and with a cut side up, in a prepared pan. Repeat to make a second roll to fill the pan. Cover lightly with plastic wrap. Repeat with the remaining dough to shape and cut two rolls to fill the second pan the same way, then cover lightly with plastic wrap.

Let the buns rise until slightly puffed, about 45 minutes. The dough will not rise much. Most of the rising happens during baking. When the dough has risen for 25 minutes, position a rack in the middle of the oven and preheat to 350°F.

Bake the buns until the tops are lightly browned and the glaze is bubbling, about 25 minutes. Let sit in the pans on wire racks for 10 minutes. Use a small, sharp knife to loosen the buns from the sides of the pans. Invert a flat serving plate on top of a pan, and holding the plate and pan firmly together with pot holders, invert them together. Carefully lift off the pan. The buns will be topped with a pretty pattern of glazed pecans. Repeat with the second pan. Serve warm or at room temperature.

The buns can be baked up to 2 days ahead, covered, and stored at room temperature. To serve, preheat the oven to 250°F and reheat the buns until warm, about 15 minutes.

CHOICES Use half of the dough, glaze, and filling and bake one pan of buns. Cover the remaining dough with plastic wrap, pressing it directly onto the surface to prevent the dough from drying out. You don't need to punch down the dough before refrigerating it. The glaze can be stored in the refrigerator and warmed to make it liquid and spreadable again.

CINNAMON BUNS WITH CREAM CHEESE GLAZE

INGREDIENTS

> *Sweet Dough for Extra-Sticky Caramel-Pecan Buns (page 71)*

Filling
> ½ cup granulated sugar
> ½ cup packed light brown sugar
> 2 tsp ground cinnamon
> ¼ tsp ground mace

> 6 tbsp unsalted butter; 4 tbsp at room temperature, 2 tbsp melted

If you like cream cheese frosting, you are going to like the frosting-like glaze that tops these buns. Also, as the buns bake, some of the cinnamon-sugar filling melts onto the bottoms of the pans and bubbles up, glazing the bottoms and sides. The result is buns glazed with sweetness from top to bottom and inside to outside. Mace is the red, lacy covering of the nutmeg seed; it has a milder flavor than nutmeg. Look for ground mace in the supermarket spice section.

METHOD Make the dough and refrigerate as directed.

Butter two 9-in round or square pans or two 11-by-7-in pans. The pans should have at least 2-in sides.

Make the filling. In a medium bowl, stir together the granulated sugar, brown sugar, cinnamon, and mace. Set aside.

Use a knife to mark the cold dough into quarters. Remove one-fourth of the dough from the refrigerator. On a floured surface, roll out the dough into a 14-by-7-in rectangle. Rolling out the dough will press out the air, so you don't need to punch it down. Cut 1 tbsp of the room-temperature butter into small pieces, and drop the pieces evenly over the rectangle. Using a thin spatula and leaving a 1-in border uncovered on all sides, spread the butter thinly over the dough. There will be some blank spaces. Sprinkle one-fourth of the filling evenly over the dough. Starting from a long side, roll up the dough tightly into a 14-in-long roll. Pinch all of the edges to seal them, and then, if necessary, pull the dough gently to extend it to 14 in. .

Using a large, sharp knife and a slight sawing motion, cut the roll crosswise into 14 equal pieces. Place the pieces, just touching and with a cut side up, in a prepared pan. Repeat to make a second roll to fill the pan. Brush the rolls with 1 tbsp of the melted butter. Sprinkle any of the sugar filling that leaked out of the buns during the transfer (and some does) to the pan over the buns. Cover lightly with plastic wrap. Repeat with the remaining dough to shape and cut two rolls to fill the second pan the same way, then cover lightly with plastic wrap.

Let the buns rise until slightly puffed, about 45 minutes. The dough will not rise much. Most of the rising happens during baking. When the dough has risen for 25 minutes, position a rack in the middle of the oven and preheat to 350°F.

Bake the buns until the tops are lightly browned and the filling is bubbling up around them, about 25 minutes. Let sit in the pans on wire racks for 5 minutes. Use a small, sharp knife to loosen the buns from the sides of the pans. Invert a wire rack on top of a pan of buns, and holding the rack and pan firmly together with pot holders, invert them together. Carefully lift off the pan and let the buns cool completely on the rack. Repeat with the second pan. Invert a flat serving plate on top of each rack of cooled buns, and holding the rack and plate firmly together, invert them.

Make the glaze. In a large bowl, and using a large spoon, stir together the butter, cream cheese, and vanilla until smoothly blended. Stir in the powdered sugar until blended, and then stir in the milk. The glaze will be thick and have the consistency of a soft frosting. Using a teaspoon, drip spoonfuls of the glaze thickly over the tops of the cooled buns. Serve at room temperature.

The glazed buns can be covered carefully and stored at room temperature overnight. To serve, preheat the oven to 225°F and reheat the buns until warm, about 15 minutes. This low temperature should not melt the glaze.

CHOICES Use half of the dough, filling, and cream cheese glaze and bake one pan of buns. Cover the remaining dough with plastic wrap, pressing it directly onto the surface to prevent the dough from drying out. You don't need to punch down the dough before refrigerating it. The glaze and the filling can be stored in the refrigerator. Just before using the glaze, add more milk as needed to return it to the proper consistency.

Cream Cheese Glaze
> *2 tbsp unsalted butter, at room temperature*
> *2 oz cream cheese, at room temperature*
> *½ tsp pure vanilla extract*
> *½ cup powdered sugar*
> *1 tbsp whole milk*

YIELD
Makes 56 small buns

MIXING TIME
20 minutes for dough, filling, and glaze

REFRIGERATOR TIME
Overnight or up to 3 days

RISING TIME
About 45 minutes after refrigeration

BAKING
350°F for about 25 minutes

AUNTIE BELL'S BUBBLE BREAD

INGREDIENTS

> 2 cups whole milk

> ½ cup shortening

> 6 to 6¼ cups unbleached all-purpose flour

> ½ cup granulated sugar

> 2 tsp kosher salt

> 4½ tsp active dry yeast (two ¼-oz packets)

> 2 large eggs

> 6 tbsp unsalted butter, melted

> 1 cup granulated sugar mixed with 1½ tsp ground cinnamon

Bubble bread is a Thanksgiving family tradition from my daughter-in-law, Kate. When Kate comes to my house for Thanksgiving, she makes the bubble bread. When I joined her family for Thanksgiving dinner, I had bubble bread made by Auntie Bell herself. It is a large bread (a given for any Thanksgiving dish) made from small balls of dough that are dipped in butter, rolled in cinnamon sugar, and stacked in a tube pan. It takes time to form, dip, and coat the "bubbles," so try to recruit a helper or two. At the table, let your guests help themselves by picking off cinnamon-glazed bubbles.

METHOD In a small saucepan, heat the milk and shortening over medium heat to about 130°F on an instant-read thermometer. Remove from the heat.

In a stand mixer fitted with the flat beater, beat together 2 cups of the flour, the sugar, salt, and yeast on low speed just until combined. Add the hot milk mixture and mix until all the ingredients are smoothly combined, then beat for 2 minutes. Stop the mixer, cover the bowl with a clean kitchen towel, and let the dough rest for 10 minutes.

Add the eggs and beat on low speed until blended. Add 4 cups of the flour and continue mixing for 5 minutes, adding up to ¼ cup more flour if needed to form a soft dough that comes away from the sides of the bowl. Stop and scrape down the bowl sides and beater as necessary. The dough is ready if when you stop the mixer and stick your finger into the dough, your finger comes out clean.

Transfer the dough to a large buttered bowl, and then turn the dough to coat it with butter on both sides. Cover the bowl with plastic wrap and refrigerate overnight or up to 2 days. The dough will about double in size.

Butter the bottom, sides, and tube of a 9½- or 10-in tube pan with at least 3¾-in sides and a fixed bottom. Line the bottom with parchment paper and butter the paper.

continued ↘

AUNTIE BELL'S BUBBLE BREAD

YIELD
Makes 1 large loaf

MIXING TIME
10 minutes

RESTING TIME
10 minutes

REFRIGERATOR TIME
Overnight or up to 2 days

RISING TIME
About 1 hour after refrigeration

BAKING
350°F for about 45 minutes

continued ↘

Put the melted butter in a small bowl and the cinnamon sugar in a second small bowl. Place a large sheet of parchment paper or waxed paper on your countertop. Remove the dough from the refrigerator and punch it down to press out the air. Using about 2 tbsp dough for each ball, form the dough into 1½-in balls. As the balls are formed, place them on the sheet of parchment. You should have about 46 balls. Dip a ball of dough in the melted butter and then roll in the cinnamon sugar to coat evenly and place in the prepared pan. Repeat with the remaining balls, spacing them about ¼ in apart to allow room for them to rise, and arranging them in three layers. The bottom layer will have about 18 balls, and the middle layer will have about 20 balls (the pan slants outward slightly). Arrange the final 8 balls on top, placing them about 1½ in in from the rim of the pan.

Cover with plastic wrap and let rise for about 1 hour. The height will not increase much, but the dough will feel lighter and will not spring back if touched lightly. When the dough has risen for 40 minutes, position a rack in the middle of the oven and preheat to 350°F.

Bake the bread until the top is browned and feels firm, about 45 minutes. Let cool in the pan on a wire rack for 15 minutes. Use a sharp knife to loosen the bread from the sides and center tube of the pan, and then turn out onto the wire rack. Peel away the paper liner. Invert a serving plate on top of the bread, and holding the rack and plate firmly together, invert them together. Lift off the rack. Serve warm or at room temperature. Let diners pick off a bubble at a time. The bubbles will separate easily.

The bread can be stored in a plastic bag at room temperature for up to 2 days. To serve, preheat the oven to 250°F and reheat the bread, covered, until warm, about 15 minutes.

CHAPTER 04
BUNS, ROLLS & SMALL BREADS

BUNS, ROLLS & SMALL BREADS

The recipes in this chapter are not just bread dough made into rolls rather than loaves, although many bread doughs can be made into smaller shapes. Instead, they are old-fashioned yeast-leavened dinner rolls; rowies, the superfast, free-form English version of a buttery, crisp croissant; and crescent-shaped butter rolls. I have also included gingerbread doughnuts and crisp, lighter-than-air beignets, both of which can be morning or dessert breads, and crumpets, which are almost as easy to make as pancakes and are better than any crumpet I have ever had, even beating out those I have sampled in tea shops in England.

Several of the rolls are shaped into round balls. I find the easiest way to produce uniform balls is to roll them between your palms. If the dough is sticky, dip your hands in flour before shaping it. Use firm pressure when rolling the dough, and continue rolling until the ball is perfectly smooth. Take the time to roll the balls of dough smoothly and you will produce rolls that will make you proud.

CHEDDAR CRACKER BREAD

INGREDIENTS

> ¾ cup unbleached all-purpose flour

> 6 oz sharp Cheddar cheese, shredded (wide holes of box grater okay)

> 4 tbsp unsalted butter, at room temperature

> 2 tsp Worcestershire sauce

> ⅛ tsp ground cayenne pepper or hot Hungarian paprika

> Sea salt or kosher salt and freshly ground black pepper for sprinkling

YIELD
Makes six 7- to 8-in rounds

MIXING TIME
10 minutes

BAKING
About 12 minutes per batch at 375°F

When I make grilled cheese sandwiches, I can never get enough of those bits of cheese that drip out from between the bread slices and cook crisply on the pan. These free-form rounds of thin cracker bread topped with salt and pepper solved the problem. Serve these cracker breads as appetizers or as an accompaniment to dishes.

METHOD Position a rack in the middle of the oven and preheat to 375°F. Have ready two baking sheets.

In a small bowl, stir together the flour and cheese. Set aside. In a large bowl, using an electric mixer on low speed, beat together the butter, Worcestershire sauce, and cayenne until blended, about 30 seconds. Add the flour mixture and beat on medium speed until a dough forms that holds together and pulls away from the sides of the bowl, about 1 minute. You will see specks of cheese in the dough.

Divide the dough into six pieces and pat each into about a 3-in disk. Wrap each in plastic wrap and refrigerate until firm, about 30 minutes.

Remove a disk of dough from the refrigerator and unwrap it. Lightly flour the work surface and the rolling pin. Place the dough disk on the floured surface and roll out into a 6-in circle. The edges do not need to be even. Cut a piece of parchment paper about 12 in long. Use a thin metal spatula to loosen the dough circle from the work surface, roll it around the rolling pin, and unroll it onto the parchment. Continue rolling out the dough circle until it has a diameter of 7 to 8 in. Lift the dough with the paper and transfer the dough to a baking sheet by inverting the paper over the baking sheet. Continue with the remaining five dough disks, placing the circles at least 1 in apart on the baking sheets. Sprinkle the dough circles lightly with salt and pepper.

Bake one sheet at time until the edges of the circles are light brown, about 12 minutes. Let cool on the pans on wire racks for 5 minutes then use a spatula to slide them onto the racks to cool completely. The cracker breads will crisp as they cool.

Cracker breads can be layered in an airtight container (preferably tin), separated by waxed paper, and stored at room temperature up to 3 days.

CRUMPETS

INGREDIENTS

> 1 cup milk, any fat content

> 1 cup water

> 1 tbsp corn or canola oil

> 1 cup unbleached all-purpose flour

> ¾ cup unbleached bread flour

> 1 tsp granulated sugar

> 1½ tsp kosher salt

> 2¼ tsp instant yeast
(one ¼-oz packet)

> Flavorless nonstick cooking spray

> 1 tsp baking soda dissolved in 1 tsp
water mixed just before cooking

> Butter for serving

YIELD
Makes 10 crumpets

MIXING TIME
10 minutes

RISING TIME
45 minutes

COOKING
About 11 minutes per batch over low heat

Crumpets are comfort food. Imagine a one-layered English muffin with a soft top dotted with small holes. These holes have one purpose: to hold the butter that melts into them when you slather the hot crumpets with soft butter.

Crumpets are cooked by pouring batter into rings on a hot griddle. You can use 3- to 4-in round cookie cutters, or you can look for crumpet rings at kitchen stores. You will probably have to cook the crumpets in two batches. While the batter waits its turn to cook it will rise, and you will have to stir it down before cooking it. You will also need to coat the rings and the griddle with cooking spray before you cook the second batch.

METHOD In a small saucepan, heat the milk, water, and oil over medium heat to about 130°F on an instant-read thermometer. Remove from the heat.

In a large bowl, and using a large spoon, stir together both flours, the sugar, salt, and yeast. Stir in the hot milk mixture, then stir vigorously for about 2 minutes to form a smooth, thick batter. Cover the bowl with plastic wrap and let the batter sit for 45 minutes. The batter will rise and become bubbly.

When the batter has risen, arrange five 3- to 4-in metal rings and about 1½ in high on a griddle. Spray the inside of each ring and the griddle with flavorless nonstick cooking spray. Heat the griddle over low heat.

Use the large spoon to stir down the batter. Gently stir in the dissolved baking soda, mixing well. Drop about ¼ cup of the batter into each hot

continued ↘

CRUMPETS

continued ↘

ring; it will spread evenly. Cook the crumpets over low heat until the bottom is browned and a firm skin has formed on top, about 10 minutes. Bubbles will form on the tops as the crumpets cook, and the tops should feel firmly baked and not sticky when touched lightly with a finger. Use tongs to lift off the rings and set them aside. If the crumpets stick to the rings (they won't if the rings are well greased), jiggle the rings gently with the tongs, and they should release. Turn the crumpets over and cook just until the second sides are firmly set, a minute or less. The insides of the crumpets will be soft. Transfer to a plate and serve, or keep warm in a low oven (250°F) while the second batch cooks. Before you cook the second batch, gently stir down the batter (it will bubble up and rise while the first batch cooks) and spray the rings and griddle again.

Serve the crumpets hot with butter.

The crumpets can be covered and stored at room temperature for up to two days. To serve, lightly toast the crumpets, buttered or not, just to warm them, or place them in a single layer on a baking sheet, cover lightly with aluminum foil, and reheat in a preheated 225°F oven just until warm, about 10 minutes.

BUTTER CRESCENTS

INGREDIENTS

> 1 cup milk, any fat content

> ½ cup unsalted butter, plus 4 tbsp melted, for brushing dough

> 5 cups unbleached all-purpose flour

> ¼ cup granulated sugar

> ¾ tsp kosher salt

> 2¼ tsp instant yeast (one ¼-oz packet)

> 3 large eggs

YIELD
Makes 32 rolls

MIXING TIME
20 minutes

RESTING TIME
10 minutes and 10 minutes

RISING TIME
45 minutes

BAKING
350°F for about 20 minutes

These are the soft, buttery American version of a French croissant.

METHOD In a small saucepan, heat the milk and ½ cup butter over medium heat to about 130°F on an instant-read thermometer.

In a stand mixer fitted with the flat beater, mix 2 cups of the flour, the sugar, salt, and yeast on low speed until combined. Mix in the hot milk mixture until combined, then beat for 2 minutes. Cover with plastic wrap and let the dough rest for 10 minutes.

On low speed, add the eggs and beat until they are blended into the dough. Add 2¾ cups of the flour and continue mixing for 5 minutes, adding up to ¼ cup flour needed to form a soft dough that comes away from the sides of the bowl. Cover the bowl with plastic wrap and let the dough rest for 10 minutes.

Line two baking sheets with parchment paper. Divide the dough into four equal pieces. Pat one piece into a thick round. On a floured work surface, roll out the dough into an 8-in circle ¼ in thick. Use a pastry brush to brush the melted butter lightly over the dough. Use a large knife to cut the circle into 8 wedges. Starting from a wide end, tightly roll up each wedge to the point. Place the wedges, point-sides down and curved slightly into crescents, on the prepared baking sheets, spacing them about 1 in apart. Lightly brush the top of each roll with a little melted butter. Repeat with the remaining dough pieces to form 32 crescents total, then cover with a clean kitchen towel.

Let the crescents rise for 45 minutes. They will not rise much. When the crescents have risen for 25 minutes, position a rack in the middle of the oven and preheat to 350°F.

Bake the crescents until the tops are browned, about 20 minutes. Use a spatula to slide them onto wire racks and brush lightly with the remaining melted butter. Serve warm or at room temperature.

The crescents can be covered and stored at room temperature. To serve, preheat the oven to 250°F and reheat the crescents, covered with aluminum foil, until warm, about 15 minutes.

BUTTERY ROWIES

INGREDIENTS

> 2¼ cups unbleached all-purpose flour

> 2 tsp kosher salt

> 2¼ tsp instant yeast (one ¼-oz packet)

> 1 cup hot water (about 130°F)

> 1 cup plus 2 tbsp unsalted butter,
  at room temperature for 20 minutes
  to soften slightly

YIELD
Makes about 20 rolls

MIXING TIME
15 minutes

RESTING TIME
15 minutes and 5 minutes

RISING TIME
About 30 minutes

BAKING
400°F for about 22 minutes

These butter-filled crisp rolls are a little-known Scottish specialty that should be famous. I first found a recipe for them in Elizabeth David's *English Bread and Yeast Cookery* and adapted my recipe from hers. Rowies are like homey croissants. Butter is folded twice into the dough to make it multilayered, but there is no chilling time as with croissant dough. The dough is quickly patted out and cut into shapes, and the layers of butter and dough are clearly visible. That means that some of the butter will melt and seep out of the rolls as they bake, so you need to use a baking sheet with 1-in sides. This is the voice of experience speaking; but even with a fire in the oven and smoke alarms blaring, I did manage to save the rowies and finish baking them later.

METHOD In a stand mixer fitted with the flat beater, mix together the flour, salt, and yeast on low speed just until combined. Add the hot water and mix just until all the ingredients are smoothly combined, then beat for 4 minutes. A soft dough will form that will come away from the sides of the bowl. Cover the bowl with a clean kitchen towel and let the dough rest for 15 minutes.

Meanwhile, cut the slightly softened butter into slices ¼ in thick. When the dough is ready, turn it out onto a floured work surface. Pat or roll the dough into a 10-by-8-in rectangle ½ in thick. Drop half of the butter slices evenly over the rectangle. Using a thin spatula and leaving a 1-in border uncovered on all sides, spread the butter evenly over the dough. With a long edge facing you, fold the dough lengthwise into thirds, and pinch the edges tightly to seal. The dough package should now measure about 3 by 8 in.

continued ↘

BUTTERY ROWIES

continued ↘

With a long edge still facing you, use a rolling pin to roll the dough gently into a 12-by-6-in rectangle. Drop the remaining butter slices evenly over the rectangle. Using the thin spatula and leaving a 1-in border uncovered on all sides, spread the butter evenly over the dough. With a short side facing you, fold the dough into thirds and pinch the edges tightly to seal. The dough package will be about 4 by 6 in. Let the dough rest for 5 minutes, which will make the final rolling easier.

Line a baking sheet with 1-in sides with parchment paper. Use the rolling pin to roll the dough gently into a 10-by-8-in rectangle ¾ in thick. Use a sharp knife to cut the dough into about 20 pieces each about 2-in square. (Or, you can cut squares about twice as large and then cut each square into two triangles.) Place the squares on the prepared baking sheet, spacing them about 1 in apart. Cover with a clean kitchen towel.

Let the rolls rise until they feel soft and puffy, about 30 minutes. The dough will not rise much. Most of the rising happens during baking. When the dough has risen for 10 minutes, position a rack in the middle of the oven and preheat to 400°F.

Bake the rolls until they are browned and crisp on the top and the bottom, about 22 minutes. Some of the butter will leak out of the rolls, so they will be baking in the bubbling butter. Let the rolls cool on the pan on a wire rack for 10 minutes to reabsorb some of the released butter. Transfer the rolls to the rack to cool slightly, about 10 minutes, then serve. The rowies taste best if eaten the same day.

The rowies can be covered and stored at room temperature for 1 day. To serve, preheat the oven to 275°F and reheat the buns, covered with aluminum foil (covering them is important or they will dry out), until warm, about 15 minutes.

SUNDAY LUNCH DINNER ROLLS

INGREDIENTS

> 1½ cups whole milk

> 4 tbsp unsalted butter, cut into pieces

> ¼ cup granulated sugar

> 4½ cups unbleached all-purpose flour

> 1 tsp kosher salt

> 2¼ tsp instant yeast (one ¼-oz packet)

> 2 large eggs

YIELD
Makes 24 rolls

MIXING TIME
10 minutes

RESTING TIME
10 minutes

RISING TIME
45 minutes

BAKING
375°F for about 20 minutes

If you were lucky enough to have a mother or grandmother who made soft, golden buttery rolls for Sunday lunches or holiday dinners, you will recognize these rolls. If not, here is a version that can be mixed in an electric mixer, has one rising in the pan, bakes in twenty minutes, and can make the memories for your family. My luck was that my friend Louisa Gerstenberger makes these classic rolls and shared her recipe with me.

METHOD Line a 15-by-10-by-1-in jelly-roll pan with parchment paper and butter the paper.

In a small saucepan, heat the milk, butter, and sugar over medium heat to about 130°F on an instant-read thermometer.

In a stand mixer fitted with the flat beater, mix together 2 cups of the flour, the salt, and the yeast on low speed just until combined. Add the hot milk mixture and mix until all the ingredients are smoothly combined, then beat for 2 minutes. Cover the bowl with plastic wrap and let the dough rest for 10 minutes.

On low speed, add the eggs and beat until incorporated. Add the remaining 2½ cups flour and continue mixing for 6 minutes. At first, the dough will look ragged, but it will become smooth after several minutes of mixing. The dough will be soft and will come away from the sides of the bowl.

Using about 2½ tbsp dough for each roll, firmly roll the dough between your palms (lightly floured if necessary) into a smooth 1¾-in ball. Place the rolls on the prepared pan, spacing them about ¾ in apart. You will have four rows of six rolls each. Cover with a clean kitchen towel.

continued ↘

SUNDAY LUNCH DINNER ROLLS

continued ↘

Let the rolls rise for 45 minutes. The rolls will look puffy and rise about 2¼ in, but most of the rising will take place during baking. When the rolls have risen for 25 minutes, position a rack in the middle of the oven and preheat to 375°F.

Bake the rolls until browned, about 20 minutes. The rolls will be touching and fill the pan. Use a spatula to slide them onto a wire rack. Serve warm or at room temperature.

The rolls can be stored in a plastic bag at room temperature for up to two days. To serve, preheat the oven to 275°F and reheat the rolls, uncovered, until warm, about 10 minutes.

GRUYÈRE & BLACK PEPPER GOUGÈRES

INGREDIENTS

> 1 cup unbleached all-purpose flour

> 1 cup water

> 6 tbsp unsalted butter, cut into pieces

> ½ tsp kosher salt

> 4 large eggs, at room temperature

> 1⅓ cups shredded Gruyère cheese

> ½ tsp freshly ground black pepper

YIELD
Makes about 40 puffs

MIXING TIME
15 minutes

BAKING
About 25 minutes per batch
at 400°F

The French *gougère*, which is made from the same dough used to make cream puffs, is flavored with Gruyère cheese and can be shaped into a single large pastry or into bite-sized puffs. Black pepper adds a zesty flavor to these small puffs. If served plain, the *gougères* should be eaten warm. But they can also be cooled and filled with crab salad, shrimp salad, egg salad, or curried or plain chicken salad and offered as hors d'oeuvres or a light main course for a spring lunch (for lunch, plan on five puffs for each serving).

As with classic cream puff dough, no leavening is included in the recipe. The steam created during baking is what makes the dough puff up, creating an open, airy texture.

METHOD Position a rack in the middle of the oven and preheat to 400°F. Line two baking sheets with parchment.

Sift the flour into a small bowl. Set aside.

In a small saucepan, combine the water, butter, and salt and bring to a boil over medium-high heat, stirring until the butter melts. Add the flour all at once and stir vigorously until the flour is incorporated and the dough pulls away from the sides of the pan in a ball. Lower the heat to medium and cook, stirring constantly, for 4 minutes. The dough will continue to pull away from the pan in a ball and, except for a customary thin film on the bottom of the pan, it will not stick to the pan.

Scrape the dough into the large bowl of a stand mixer fitted with the flat beater and beat on medium speed until the dough forms large clumps, about 1 minute. Add the eggs, one at a time, and beat until completely blended before adding the next egg, about 1 minute for each egg. On low speed, mix in the cheese and pepper until incorporated.

Using an ice cream scoop with a 1-tbsp capacity or two spoons (one to measure and one to push the dough onto the pans), drop mounds of the dough onto the prepared pans, spacing them about 2 in apart. If the mounds are irregular, use a wet finger to smooth the dough.

Bake one sheet at a time until the puffs are lightly browned, about 25 minutes. Let cool on the pans on wire racks for 5 to 10 minutes, then serve warm.

The puffs can be covered and stored at room temperature for up to two days. To serve, preheat the oven to 325°F and reheat the puffs, uncovered, until warm, about 5 minutes.

GINGERBREAD DOUGHNUTS WITH LEMON GLAZE

INGREDIENTS

> 2¼ cups unbleached all-purpose flour
> 2 tsp ground ginger
> 1½ tsp ground cinnamon
> ¼ tsp ground cloves
> ½ tsp baking powder
> ½ tsp baking soda
> ½ tsp kosher salt
> 1 large egg
> ½ cup packed dark brown sugar
> 1 tbsp unsulfured light molasses
> ½ cup buttermilk, any fat content
> Corn or canola oil for deep-frying

I live in doughnut country. In my village of Camden, Maine, the story—or legend—goes that Hanson Crockett Gregory made the first hole in the doughnut in 1847. Gregory reportedly worked in a Camden bakery, where he knocked out the under-cooked centers of doughnuts that were to be filled with jelly. A few miles down the road from Camden lies Thomaston, Maine, where the first doughnut-hole machine was patented in 1872 by John Blondel. Many of our traditional New England dough-nuts are flavored with spices, and these have the spices and dark color of a good New England gingerbread.

As with the beignets on page 96, a deep-frying thermometer comes in handy for keeping the temperature of the frying oil constant. The doughnuts triple in size in the hot oil, growing from a raw dough ring just ½ in thick to a cooked doughnut about 1½ in thick.

METHOD Sift together the flour, ginger, cinnamon, cloves, baking powder, baking soda and salt into a medium bowl. Set aside.

In a stand mixer fitted with the flat beater, beat together the egg and brown sugar on low speed until blended. Add the molasses and butter-milk and beat until blended. Mix in the flour mixture until thoroughly incorporated and a soft dough forms that holds together. The dough will be sticky.

Flour a work surface and a rolling pin. (Flour the work surface carefully to keep the sticky dough from adhering to it.) Transfer the dough to the work surface and roll out into a 9-in circle ½ in thick. Using a 2¾-in doughnut cutter, cut out 9 doughnuts.

Or, use a 2¾-in biscuit cutter to cut out circles, and then use a ½-in cutter (the round wide end of a pastry tip works well) to cut out a hole in the center of each circle.

Line a baking sheet with paper towels. Pour 2 in of oil into a heavy, medium saucepan and heat over medium heat to 365°F on a deep-frying thermometer. Add two or three doughnuts and their holes to the hot oil and fry until the undersides of the doughnuts are light brown, about 2½ minutes. The doughnuts and holes will puff and float to the top. Using a slotted spoon, turn the doughnuts and holes and fry on the second sides to a light brown, about 1½ minutes. Using the slotted spoon, transfer the doughnuts to the towel-lined pan to drain. Repeat with the remaining doughnuts, checking to make sure the oil is at 365°F before you add more doughnuts and keeping the temperature of the oil steady throughout the frying. Let the doughnuts cool slightly while you make the glaze.

Make the glaze. In a medium bowl, mix together the lemon juice and zest. Add the powdered sugar and 1 tsp milk and stir to make a smooth, thick glaze, adding a few more drops of milk, if necessary.

Dip the top of each warm doughnut and doughnut hole in the glaze, and use a thin metal spatula to spread it evenly over the top.

Serve the doughnuts at room temperature the day they are made.

CHOICES A cinnamon glaze can be substituted for the lemon glaze. Omit the lemon juice and lemon zest, add ½ tsp ground cinnamon, and use enough milk, about 2½ tbsp, to make a smooth, thick glaze.

Lemon Glaze
> *2 tbsp fresh lemon juice*
> *1 tsp grated lemon zest*
> *1 cup powdered sugar*
> *1 tsp milk, any fat content, or more if needed*

YIELD
Makes 9 doughnuts and 9 doughnut holes

MIXING TIME
10 minutes

FRYING
About 4 minutes per batch at 365°F

CINNAMON BEIGNETS

INGREDIENTS

> ½ cup granulated sugar plus 1½ tbsp

> ¾ tsp ground cinnamon

> ½ cup unbleached all-purpose flour

> ½ cup water

> 4 tbsp unsalted butter, cut into pieces

> 1 tsp kosher salt

> 2 large eggs, at room temperature

> 1 tsp pure vanilla extract

> Corn or canola oil for deep-frying

YIELD
Makes about 15 beignets

MIXING TIME
10 minutes

FRYING
About 7 minutes per batch
at 350°F

French beignets, Italian *zeppole*, American fritters—whatever the name, the result is the same: crisp, airy deep-fried puffs that fall into the bet-you-can't-eat-just-one category. Price Kushner, who with Melissa Kelley owns Primo restaurant in Rockland, Maine, shared his perfect recipe with me.

To form nicely rounded beignets, use an ice cream scoop, or for irregularly shaped beignets, use two tablespoons, one to scoop the dough and one to push it into the oil. If the frying oil is kept at 350°F, the beignets will come out crisp and not at all greasy. A deep-frying thermometer for measuring the temperature of the oil guarantees perfect frying every time. If you don't have one, the small investment is worth the consistent results.

METHOD In a medium bowl, stir together the ½ cup sugar and the cinnamon. Set aside. Sift the flour into a small bowl. Set aside.

In a small saucepan, combine the water, butter, salt, and the remaining 1½ tbsp sugar and bring to a boil over medium-high heat, stirring until the butter melts. Add the flour all at once and stir vigorously until the flour is incorporated and the dough pulls away from the sides of the pan in a ball. Lower the heat to medium and cook, stirring constantly, for 4 minutes. The dough will continue to pull away from the sides of the pan in a ball and, except for a customary thin film on the bottom of the pan, it will not stick to the pan.

Scrape the dough into the large bowl of a stand mixer fitted with the flat beater and beat on medium speed until the dough forms large clumps, about 1 minute. Add one of the eggs and the vanilla and beat until the egg is smoothly blended into the dough, about 1 minute. Add the remaining

continued ↘

CINNAMON BEIGNETS

continued ↘

egg and beat until smoothly blended, about 1 minute. Use immediately, or cover with plastic wrap, pressing it directly onto the surface of the dough. The dough can be left at room temperature for up to 1 hour before using.

Line a baking sheet with paper towels. Pour 2 in of oil into a heavy, medium saucepan and heat over medium-high heat to 350°F on a deep-frying thermometer. Using an ice cream scoop with a 1-tbsp capacity or two spoons (one to measure and one to push the dough into the oil), drop 7 or 8 spoonfuls of dough into the hot oil and fry for about 7 minutes. The beignets will float to the top almost immediately, and as they cook, they will almost double in size. Use a slotted spoon to turn the beignets occasionally so they are an even golden brown on all sides. When they are ready, use the slotted spoon to transfer them to the towel-lined pan to drain.

Roll the hot beignets in the cinnamon sugar and transfer to a serving plate. Fry the remaining dough the same way, checking to make sure the oil is at 350°F before you add the spoonfuls of dough to the pan and keeping the temperature of the oil steady throughout the frying. Then drain and roll in the cinnamon sugar.

Serve the warm beignets immediately.

The beignets can be kept at room temperature for 2 hours and then reheated, uncovered, in a preheated 250°F oven just until they are warm, about 10 minutes.

CHAPTER 05
LOAVES & ROUNDS

LOAVES & ROUNDS

I was mixing a Sally Lunn bread, a classic batter bread, in my stand mixer when the "Eureka!" moment hit. Why not turn my bread dough recipes into easy-mix batter bread recipes? Batter breads are yeast breads that have less flour in proportion to liquid than ordinary yeast breads and can be mixed quickly with an electric mixer, in a food processor, or by hand. Stirring by hand, as is the case with any batter, is a bit more work, of course, but it is certainly an option. The doughs, rather than being fairly firm, are thick, elastic, stretchy batters, and somewhat sticky.

I began my experiments by increasing the liquid in a traditionally firm dough to create a softer batter-type dough. As I worked, I developed a simple test for when the dough was sticky but not too sticky: I stuck a clean finger into it. If the dough felt sticky but my finger came out clean, the dough was just right. The results of my experiments became these easy-mixing, baker-friendly yeast breads. Eureka!

Mixing a batter bread is as simple as stirring the dry ingredients and yeast together, adding the wet ingredients, and beating, processing, or stirring the dough to aerate it and develop the gluten. In other words, to get things moving, I usually mix in the flour in two additions, one with the liquids and one after the liquids have been incorporated. This makes the first mixing a breeze, even by hand, and allows adjustment of the final addition of flour and liquid to achieve the perfect consistency.

To make a batter bread in a food processor, mix all of the ingredients as directed for a stand mixer. After adding the final portion of flour, process for 30 seconds to mix and beat the dough. The dough should be smooth. If the amount of dough is too large for the work bowl, divide the dough in half and beat each half separately. If, as you beat, the dough covers the top of the blade and slows the machine, stop the processor and scrape down the dough.

Some of the recipes in this chapter are leavened with baking powder or baking soda, including Borrowdale Raisin Tea Loaf (page 101); Carrot, Cranberry & Walnut Loaf (page 104); and Dark Irish Soda Bread (page 105). The first two are cake-type batters, and the latter, a whole-wheat version of the Irish classic, is made with baking soda, but has a slightly crumbly texture reminiscent of yeast bread.

BORROWDALE RAISIN TEA LOAF

INGREDIENTS

> *2 cups raisins*

> *1¼ cups hot black tea (not flavored or herb)*

> *1½ cups whole-wheat flour*

> *1 tsp baking soda*

> *¼ tsp kosher salt*

> *¾ cup packed dark brown sugar*

> *1 large egg*

> *1 tsp grated orange zest*

YIELD
Makes 1 loaf

MIXING TIME
10 minutes

BAKING
350°F for about 45 minutes

When my Scottish neighbor, Graham Phaup, got a yen for the tea bread of his schooldays, he called his friend Ellodie in England, for the recipe. I live on a dead-end street in a close-knit community, so once Graham baked the tea bread, I heard the news quickly. Soon a plate of the bread took the short trip down to my house. The batter is mixed with tea-soaked raisins and whole-wheat flour, which turns the light-textured bread an appealing brown and gives it a subtle flavor. It is the perfect bread with, of course, a nice cuppa tea. You'll need to plan ahead here: the raisins must be soaked overnight.

METHOD Put the raisins in a medium bowl and pour the hot tea over them. Cover and let sit at room temperature overnight.

Position a rack in the middle of the oven and preheat to 350°F. Butter a 9-by-5-by-3-in loaf pan (or other loaf pan with an 8-cup capacity). Line the bottom of the pan with parchment paper and butter the paper.

Sift together the flour, baking soda, and salt into a medium bowl. Set aside.

In a stand mixer fitted with the flat beater, beat together the sugar, egg, and orange zest on medium speed until well blended and smooth, about 1 minute. On low speed, mix in the flour mixture just to incorporate it. Mix in the raisins and any tea remaining in the bowl, mixing until evenly blended. Scrape the batter into the prepared pan.

Bake until the top feels firm if lightly touched and a toothpick inserted in the center comes out clean, about 45 minutes. Let cool in the pan on a wire rack for about 10 minutes. Run a small, sharp knife around the inside edge of the pan to loosen the bread sides, then turn the bread out onto the rack. Peel off the parchment. Let cool completely.

The tea bread can be wrapped with plastic wrap and stored at room temperature up to 2 days.

BUTTERMILK SANDWICH LOAF

INGREDIENTS

> 1¼ cups buttermilk, any fat content

> 2 tbsp unsalted butter, plus 2 tsp melted, for brushing top of loaf

> 3¼ cups unbleached all-purpose flour

> 1 tbsp granulated sugar

> 1 tbsp wheat bran

> 1 tsp kosher salt

> 2¼ tsp instant yeast (one ¼-oz packet)

> 1 large egg

YIELD
Makes 1 large loaf

MIXING TIME
15 minutes

RISING TIME
About 25 minutes

BAKING
375°F for about 40 minutes

Ideal for sandwiches, toast, or savory bread pudding, this golden batter bread is a good bet to become a daily fixture on your menu. The dough rises a lot and the finished loaf is quite rounded and full and bigger than you might expect from a standard loaf pan.

METHOD Butter a 9-by-5-by-3-in loaf pan (or other loaf pan with an 8-cup capacity).

In a small saucepan, heat the buttermilk and 2 tbsp butter over medium heat to about 130°F on an instant-read thermometer. Remove from the heat.

In a stand mixer fitted with the flat beater, mix together 1½ cups of the flour, the sugar, wheat bran, salt, and yeast on low speed just until combined. Add the hot buttermilk mixture and mix until all the ingredients are smoothly combined. Add the egg and continue beating for 1 minute. Add the remaining 1¾ cups flour and continue mixing for 5 minutes. The dough will be sticky and will not come away from the sides of the bowl. Scrape the dough into the prepared pan and brush the top with the melted butter.

Cover the pan loosely with waxed paper and let the dough rise to within 1 in of the top of the pan, about 25 minutes. When the dough has risen for 5 minutes, position a rack in the middle of the oven and preheat to 375°F.

Bake until the top feels firm and is lightly browned, about 40 minutes. Let cool in the pan on a wire rack for 10 minutes, then turn out onto the rack and let cool completely.

The bread can be stored in a plastic bag at room temperature for up to 2 days.

CHOICES Add 2 tsp grated orange or lemon zest to the dough with the liquids.

CARROT, CRANBERRY & WALNUT LOAF

As every admirer of it already knows, the carrot cake is one good cake. This slightly sweet carrot loaf, which includes fresh cranberries and whole-wheat flour, has the same carrot cake appeal but with a nice dose of vitamins.

METHOD Position a rack in the middle of the oven and preheat to 350°F. Butter a 9-by-5-by-3-in loaf pan (or other loaf pan with an 8-cup capactiy). Line the bottom of the pan with parchment paper.

In a large bowl, and using a large spoon, stir together both flours, the sugar, baking powder, cinnamon, and salt. Add the eggs, oil, carrots, vanilla, and ginger and stir just until completely incorporated with the flour mixture. Stir in the walnuts and cranberries. Scrape the batter into the prepared pan.

Bake until the top feels firm if lightly touched and a toothpick inserted in the center comes out clean, about 55 minutes. Let cool in the pan on a wire rack for about 10 minutes. Run a small, sharp knife around the inside edge of the pan to loosen the bread sides, then turn the bread out onto the rack. Peel off the parchment. Let cool completely.

The carrot bread can be wrapped in plastic wrap and stored at room temperature for up to 3 days.

INGREDIENTS

> 1 cup unbleached all-purpose flour
> 1 cup whole-wheat flour
> 1 cup granulated sugar
> 1 tsp baking powder
> 1 tsp ground cinnamon
> ¼ tsp kosher salt
> 3 large eggs, lightly beaten
> ¾ cup corn or canola oil
> 1½ cups coarsely grated carrots
> 1 tsp pure vanilla extract
> ½ tsp finely grated, peeled fresh ginger
> ¾ cup coarsely chopped walnuts
> ¾ cup fresh or thawed, frozen cranberries, coarsely chopped

YIELD
Makes 1 loaf

MIXING TIME
10 minutes

BAKING
350°F for about 55 minutes

DARK IRISH SODA BREAD

INGREDIENTS

> 1½ cups whole-wheat flour

> ¾ cup unbleached all-purpose flour

> 1 tbsp packed dark or light brown sugar

> 2 tsp caraway seeds

> 1 tsp baking soda

> ½ tsp kosher salt

> 2 tbsp unsalted butter, melted

> 1 tbsp unsulfured light molasses

> 1 cup buttermilk, any fat content

YIELD
Makes one 8-in oval loaf

MIXING TIME
10 minutes

BAKING
375°F for about 35 minutes

Several years ago, my husband and I took a driving trip around the southern coast of Ireland, and we enjoyed delicious bread wherever we ate. I was looking forward to Irish bread made with baking soda, but we were always served crusty, light-textured yeast breads—or so I thought. One evening, after being served a dark whole-wheat loaf, I asked the waiter if any soda bread was available and was told that I was eating exactly that. That night I discovered that I had just spent ten days enjoying Irish soda bread.

METHOD Position a rack in the middle of the oven and preheat to 375°F. Butter a baking sheet and sprinkle it lightly with whole-wheat flour.

In a stand mixer fitted with the flat beater, mix together both flours, the brown sugar, caraway seeds, baking soda, and salt on low speed just until combined. Add the melted butter and mix until blended. Stir the molasses into the buttermilk, add to the flour mixture, and continue mixing on low speed until a soft dough forms, about 1 minute.

Gather up the dough into a ball and roll it around between your palms to smooth it as much as possible. It will not be perfectly smooth. Form into an 8-in-long oval by patting it gently and place on the prepared pan. Use a sharp knife to cut a lengthwise slash about 5 in long and ¼ in deep along the center of the loaf.

Bake the bread until it feels firm and crisp and the bottom is browned if you lift it carefully, about 35 minutes. Let cool on the pan on a wire rack for 10 minutes; then slide onto the rack and let cool completely.

The bread is best when served the same day it is baked. It can be sliced and toasted the next day.

TOASTED WALNUT & DATE WHOLE-WHEAT ROUND

INGREDIENTS
> *Unsalted butter for pan*
> *2 cups whole-wheat flour*
> *1 tbsp packed light brown sugar*
> *1 tsp kosher salt*
> *2¼ tsp instant yeast (one ¼-oz packet)*
> *1 cup hot water (about 130°F)*
> *1 cup pitted dates, preferably Medjool, halved*
> *1 cup walnut halves, toasted (page 13)*

YIELD
Makes one 9-in round

MIXING TIME
10 minutes

RISING TIME
About 30 minutes

BAKING
375°F for about 35 minutes

Whole-wheat flour adds an appealing light brown color and, of course, lots of nutrition to this loaf. Large pieces of Medjool dates and walnuts poke out of the top and contribute a noticeable chewy, crunchy texture. Big Medjool dates are soft and easily pitted. The bread bakes in a shallow round pan that encourages a crisp crust all over the loaf. For a softer crust, bake it in a loaf pan or deep baking dish.

METHOD Butter a 9-in round layer pan or baking dish with 2-in sides and sprinkle the bottom lightly with whole-wheat flour.

In a stand mixer fitted with the flat beater, mix together the flour, brown sugar, salt, and yeast on low speed just until combined. Add the hot water and continue mixing until the dough begins to come away from the sides of the bowl, about 2 minutes. Add the dates and walnuts and continue mixing for 5 minutes, stopping to scrape down the beater if necessary. The dough should be soft and if you stop the mixer and stick a finger into the dough, your finger will come out clean.

Gather up the dough into a ball and roll it around between your palms until smooth; then form into an 8-in ball. Place it in the prepared pan. The dough will not touch the edges of the pan. Use a sharp knife to cut a cross about 6 in long and ¼ in deep in the top of the dough. Sprinkle the top lightly with flour.

Cover the pan with plastic wrap and let the dough rise until it fills the pan, about 30 minutes. When the dough has risen for 10 minutes, position a rack in the middle of the oven and preheat to 375°F.

Bake the bread until the top feels firm and is lightly browned, about 35 minutes. Let cool in the pan on a wire rack for 10 minutes, then turn out onto the rack and let cool completely.

The bread can be stored in a plastic bag at room temperature for up to 2 days.

CHOICES Substitute pecan halves for the walnuts, and dried figs, cut in half, for the dates.

AN EVERYDAY CRUSTY ROUND OR TWO

INGREDIENTS

> Stone-ground yellow cornmeal for pan
> 3½ cups unbleached all-purpose flour
> ½ cup whole-wheat flour
> 1 tbsp wheat bran
> 1½ tsp kosher salt
> 2¼ tsp instant yeast
  (one ¼-oz packet)
> 2 cups hot water (about 130°F)

YIELD
Makes one 9-in round or two
6-in one rounds

MIXING TIME
15 minutes

RISING TIME
About 40 minutes

BAKING
450°F for about 25 minutes for the
large round or about 22 minutes for
the small rounds

Here is all you have to do to make this light wheat bread: Combine all-purpose flour, whole-wheat flour, wheat bran, salt, and yeast. Mix in hot water and then knead by mixing with an electric mixer or by stirring with a wooden spoon for about 5 minutes. Form the dough into one or two rounds, let it rise, and then bake. In about 1½ hours, the whole house will smell like freshly baked bread—bread to make any baker burst with pride. Applause now.

This dough is very sticky and soft. When you scrape it out onto the floured work surface, it sort of waddles out of the bowl. This is good. Lift and flour it on both sides and then shape it. It is soft and a pleasure to form.

METHOD Sprinkle a baking sheet with cornmeal and all-purpose flour.

In a stand mixer fitted with the flat beater, mix together both flours, the wheat bran, salt, and yeast on low speed just until combined. Add the hot water and continue mixing for 5 minutes. The dough will be sticky and will not come away from the sides of the bowl.

Scrape the dough onto a generously floured work surface (a plastic dough scraper is handy for getting it out of the bowl). Flour your hands and turn the dough once to flour both sides. Form the dough into a ball and then gently pull and fold the dough under itself, turning it three or four times in your hands to form a smooth top and a 6-in round. Put the dough on the prepared pan. Or, divide the dough in half, form two 5-in rounds, and place about 5 in apart on the prepared pan. Sprinkle the top of the dough lightly with all-purpose flour to prevent the paper from sticking during rising, then cover loosely with waxed paper.

Let the dough rise until it is about ½ in taller and has spread 1½ to 3 in, about 25 minutes. Using a small, sharp knife or a single-edge razor blade, cut three parallel slashes across the top of the round(s), each about 3 in long, ¼ in deep, and spaced about 2 in apart. Let rise for 15 minutes more.

When the dough has risen for 20 minutes, position a rack in the middle of the oven and preheat to 450°F. When the dough has risen for 30 minutes, put a clean rock on a metal pie pan and put the pan on the lowest rack of the oven (or, lacking a rock, put the empty pan on the rack).

When the bread is ready to go into the oven, pour about 2 tbsp water over the rock in the pie pan to create steam and encourage a crisp crust. Bake the bread until the top feels firm and is browned, about 25 minutes for a large round or about 22 minutes for the smaller rounds. The bread will rise about 2 in during baking. Transfer the bread to a wire rack and let cool completely.

The bread can be stored in a paper bag at room temperature for up to 3 days. If the bread is cut, wrap a piece of plastic wrap around the cut end before slipping it into the bag. To reheat the bread before it is cut, preheat the oven to 275°F, place the loaf directly on the oven rack, and heat until the crust is crisp and feels warm, about 10 minutes.

CHOICES This bread makes good garlic bread. Spread thick slices of the bread with Thyme-Garlic Butter (page 139), wrap in aluminum foil, and heat in a preheated 300°F oven for about 20 minutes.

LOTS OF CHEESE BREAD

INGREDIENTS

> Unsalted butter for pan

> 1 cup whole milk

> 2¾ cups unbleached all-purpose flour

> 1 tbsp granulated sugar

> ½ tsp kosher salt

> 2¼ tsp instant yeast (one ¼-oz packet)

> 1 large egg

> 8 oz sharp Cheddar cheese, cut into ½- to ¾-in pieces

YIELD
Makes 1 large loaf

MIXING TIME
10 minutes

RISING TIME
About 45 minutes

BAKING
375°F for about 45 minutes

Cubes of sharp Cheddar form pockets of melted cheese and a crisp, browned cheese crust all around this loaf. Use this bread to make the best grilled cheese panini (see page 135) you will ever taste.

METHOD Butter a 9-by-5-by-3-in loaf pan (or other loaf pan with an 8-cup capacity). Line the bottom of the pan with parchment paper.

In a small saucepan, heat the milk over medium heat to about 130°F on an instant-read thermometer. Remove from the heat.

In a stand mixer fitted with the flat beater, mix together 1 cup of the flour, the sugar, salt, and yeast on low speed just until combined. Add the hot milk and mix until smoothly combined. Add the egg and continue beating for 2 minutes. Add the remaining 1¾ cups flour and continue mixing for 5 minutes. The dough will be soft and will come away from the sides of the bowl, and if you stop the mixer and stick a finger into the dough, your finger will come out clean.

Scrape the dough onto a lightly floured work surface. Sprinkle the cheese pieces evenly over the top. Using the heel of one hand, push the dough down and away against the surface. Then, using your fingertips, fold it toward you. Rotate the dough a quarter turn and repeat the pushing and folding about five times. Several pieces of cheese will poke out of the dough. This is fine. The dough will firm slightly as the cheese is worked into it. Use your hands to pat the dough into a loaf that will fit in the prepared pan. The loaf will not completely fill the pan.

Cover the pan with plastic wrap and let the dough rise to within 1 in of the top of the pan, about 45 minutes. When the dough has risen for 25 minutes, position a rack in the middle of the oven and preheat to 375°F.

Bake the bread until the top feels firm and is lightly browned, about 45 minutes. Let cool in the pan on a wire rack for 10 minutes. Run a small, sharp knife around the inside edge of the pan to loosen the bread sides, then turn the bread out onto the rack. Let cool completely.

The bread can be stored in a plastic bag at room temperature for up to 3 days.

SALLY LUNN BREAD

INGREDIENTS

> 1¼ cups milk, any fat content

> ½ cup unsalted butter

> 4 cups unbleached all-purpose flour

> ⅓ cup granulated sugar

> 1 tsp kosher salt

> 2¼ tsp instant yeast (one ¼-oz packet)

> 3 large eggs

YIELD
Makes 1 large round or 2 loaves

MIXING TIME
10 minutes

RESTING TIME
10 minutes

RISING TIME
About 1 hour

BAKING
375°F for about 50 minutes

Never has so little effort produced such a tremendous bread. This batter bread, easily mixed in a mixer or by hand (the mixing time is about the same), bakes up into a rich, yellow, light-textured, close-grained round. I bake it in a large tube pan, but you can use two loaf pans. Stories abound on its origin: was it named for Sally Lunn, the daughter of a pastry chef in Bath, England; or is the name a corruption of the French *sol et lune* (sun and moon) and the bread the creation of a French Huguenot baker? There is agreement, however, on how the bread gets its cakelike character: plenty of butter, milk, and eggs.

METHOD Butter the bottom, sides, and tube of a 9½- or 10-in tube pan with at least 3¾-in sides and a fixed bottom. Line the bottom with parchment paper and butter the paper. Or, butter two 9-by-5-by-3-in loaf pans, line the bottoms with parchment, and butter the paper.

In a small saucepan, heat the milk and butter over medium heat to about 130°F on an instant-read thermometer. Remove from the heat.

In a stand mixer fitted with the flat beater, mix together 1 cup of the flour, the sugar, salt, and yeast on low speed just until combined. Add the hot milk mixture and mix until all the ingredients are smoothly combined. Cover the bowl with a clean kitchen towel and let the dough rest for 10 minutes.

Add the eggs and mix on low speed until combined, then continue to beat for 1 minute. Add the remaining 3 cups flour and continue mixing for 6 minutes. The dough will be sticky and will not come away from the sides of the bowl. Scrape the dough into the prepared pan(s).

Cover the pan(s) with plastic wrap and let the dough rise for about 1 hour. The dough will rise about halfway up the sides of the pan(s). When the dough has risen for 40 minutes, position a rack in the middle of the oven and preheat to 375°F.

Bake the bread until the top feels firm and the top and sides are browned, about 50 minutes. The bread will rise to at least the top of the pan(s). Let cool in the pan(s) on a wire rack for 10 minutes. Then turn out onto the rack, peel off the parchment, and let cool completely.

The bread can be stored in a plastic bag at room temperature for up to 3 days.

TOMATO, BASIL & ONION FOCACCIA & FIG & GORGONZOLA FOCACCIA

INGREDIENTS

Focaccia Dough
> 2½ cups unbleached bread flour
> ½ tsp kosher salt
> 2¼ tsp instant yeast
  (one ¼-oz packet)
> 1 cup hot water
  (about 130°F)
> 2 tbsp extra-virgin olive oil

Tomato, Basil & Onion Topping
> 3 tbsp extra-virgin olive oil
> 1 tomato, sliced through the stem end
> 2 tbsp lightly packed
  fresh basil leaves, torn into strips
> ½ medium yellow onion, thinly sliced

Focaccia is the middle ground between pizza and traditional bread. The best versions taste of good olive oil, which is typically brushed on the pan and on the top of the dough and sometimes drizzled on the toppings. The latter can be as simple as salt and herbs or as complex as an array of vegetables, cheeses, and/or meats. Here are two of my favorite combinations: tomato, basil, and onion, and fig and Gorgonzola cheese. If you prefer to make two focaccie with the same topping, the ingredients for both toppings double easily.

You can serve small wedges of focaccia for appetizers and large wedges to accompany a supper main course. Room-temperature focaccia makes great picnic fare.

METHOD Oil two 8-in round pans or baking dishes with 2-in sides or a rimmed baking sheet with extra-virgin olive oil. (Round pans will yield a thicker focaccia, and the baking sheet a thinner focaccia with crisp edges.)

Make the dough. In a stand mixer fitted with the flat beater, mix together 1 cup of the flour, the salt, and the yeast on low speed just until combined. Add the hot water and olive oil and continue mixing for 1 minute. Add the remaining 1½ cups flour and continue mixing for 4 minutes. The dough will be soft but will come away from the sides of the bowl. Cover the bowl with a clean kitchen towel and let the dough rest for 10 minutes.

Divide the dough in half, and form each half into a ball. On a lightly floured work surface, roll out half of the dough into an 8-in circle ½ in thick. Transfer to a prepared round pan or the baking sheet. Repeat

continued ↘

TOMATO, BASIL & ONION FOCACCIA & FIG & GORGONZOLA FOCACCIA

Fig & Gorgonzola Topping

> *3 tbsp extra-virgin olive oil*

> *1 large clove garlic, minced*

> *½ cup dried Calimyrna or Black Mission figs, stemmed and cut into ¼-in pieces*

> *1 oz Gorgonzola cheese, crumbled*

> *½ yellow onion, thinly sliced (optional)*

> *Freshly ground black pepper*

YIELD
Makes two 8- to 9-in focaccie

MIXING TIME
15 minutes

RESTING TIME
10 minutes

RISING TIME
About 30 minutes

BAKING
475°F for 16 to 18 minutes

continued ↘

with the remaining half of the dough and transfer to the second prepared round pan or to the baking sheet.

Add the tomato topping. Using a pastry brush, brush the top of one dough circle generously with some of the olive oil. Leaving a ½-in border uncovered around the entire edge, arrange the tomato slices over the oiled circle, then sprinkle the basil over the tomato. Drizzle some of the remaining olive oil over the basil. Arrange the onion slices over the basil and drizzle the remaining olive oil over the covered dough circle, letting some drip down the sides.

Add the fig and cheese topping. Using a pastry brush, brush the top of the second dough circle generously with some of the olive oil. Leaving a ½-in border uncovered around the entire edge, sprinkle the garlic over the oiled circle. Arrange the fig pieces over the garlic. Sprinkle the cheese and onion slices (if using) evenly over the figs. Grind black pepper over the top. Drizzle the remaining olive oil over the dough circle, letting some drip down the sides.

Cover the topped dough circles with a clean kitchen towel and let rise for about 30 minutes. The dough will rise slightly and look puffy. Most of the rising takes place during baking. When the dough has risen for 10 minutes, position a rack in the middle of the oven and preheat to 475°F.

Bake until the edges are well browned, the topping is cooked, and any cheese is melted, about 16 minutes for the baking sheet and 18 minutes for the baking pans. Let cool in the pan(s) on a wire rack for 5 minutes, then cut into wedges and serve hot.

CHAPTER 06
BREAD DISHES & BREAD TOPPINGS

BREAD DISHES
& BREAD TOPPINGS

Good bread is too good to waste even a crumb of it. After a couple of days, a bread may not be at its best to serve as fresh bread, but it is now at the perfect stage to become the most important ingredient in another dish. Bread can thicken soups, become the toasted base for a sweet almond custard, or be the main ingredient for a corn bread salad. We have all tasted bread pudding, but making it with your homemade Sally Lunn Bread (page 112) or Brioche (page 56) and topping it with sweetened bread crumbs from the same loaf produces a bread pudding (see page 136) that won't soon be forgotten. Homemade rolls or breads make the best sliders, muffaletta, and panini. Best of all, most of these "waste not, want not" dishes can be made hours or even a day ahead of serving.

At the end of this chapter, you will find a lot of new ideas for topping breads, including sweet and savory butters, a fruit sauce and a fruit compote, a pair of flavored whipped creams, and a creamy English lemon curd that tastes great on everything from scones to popovers to morning toast.

HAM & SWISS ON RYE STRATA

INGREDIENTS

> Unsalted butter for baking dish
> 12 slices Dark Rye Bread (page 58)
> 3 tbsp Dijon mustard
> 8 oz baked ham, sliced
> 8 oz Swiss cheese, coarsely shredded
> 2 cups whole milk
> 6 large eggs
> ⅛ tsp kosher salt
> ¼ tsp freshly ground black pepper
> Dijon mustard for serving

YIELD

Makes 8 servings

The classic *strata* is a brunch dish in which bread, a simple egg-milk custard, and cheese are layered and then baked. In this recipe, ham, Swiss cheese, mustard, and rye bread turn a favorite sandwich combination into a make-ahead *strata*. The layers go together quickly and at your convenience, and then can be baked in little more than half an hour for brunch, lunch, or dinner.

METHOD Generously butter a 13-by-9-by-2-in baking dish. Spread one side of the bread slices with the mustard. Arrange 6 slices of the bread in a single layer on the bottom of the prepared baking dish. They can over-lap slightly if necessary. Spread half of the ham on top of the bread, and sprinkle with half of the cheese. Repeat the layers with the remaining bread, ham, and cheese. In a medium bowl, whisk together the milk, eggs, salt, and pepper until blended. Slowly pour the milk mixture evenly over the layers. Cover and refrigerate for at least 4 hours or up to overnight.

Preheat the oven to 350°F.

Bake the *strata* until the cheese melts and begins to bubble and the top is puffed and looks set, about 35 minutes.

Remove from the oven and let sit for 10 minutes. Serve directly from the dish. Pass mustard at the table to spread on each serving.

BAKED ALMOND BRIOCHE TOAST

INGREDIENTS

> ½ cup whole natural almonds, toasted (see page 13)

> ¼ cup powdered sugar

> ½ cup unsalted butter, at room temperature

> ½ cup granulated sugar

> 2 large eggs

> 8 loaf-sized slices 1- or 2-day-old Brioche (page 56), each about ¾ in thick

> ½ cup natural or blanched sliced almonds

YIELD
Makes 8 toasts

BAKING TIME
350° F for about 15 minutes

These toasts, which are spread with almond cream and topped with crunchy almonds, began as a way for thrifty French bakers to use up unsold brioche. With good reason, the toasts became so popular that brioche now is often baked in order to make the almond toasts. If using a large, round brioche, cut the large slices in half, to make them loaf size.

METHOD Position a rack in the middle of the oven and preheat to 350°F. Line a baking sheet with parchment paper.

In a food processor, combine the whole almonds and powdered sugar and process until the nuts are finely ground. Transfer the ground nut mixture to a small bowl. Add the butter and granulated sugar to the processor (no need to clean it first) and process until creamy, about 20 seconds. With the processor running, add the eggs one at a time and process until blended and smooth, about 20 seconds. Add the ground nut mixture and process just until incorporated, 20 seconds or less. You will have about 1½ cups almond cream.

Place the bread slices 1 in apart on the prepared pan. Leaving a ½-in border uncovered on all sides, spread about 3 tbsp almond cream over the top of each slice. Sprinkle the top of each slice with 1 tbsp of the sliced almonds.

Bake until the tops are lightly browned and the bottoms are toasted and browned, about 15 minutes. Let cool on the pan on a wire rack. Serve the toasts warm or at room temperature the same day they are baked.

The almond cream can be prepared a day ahead, covered, and refrigerated. Before using, let the almond cream sit at room temperature until it can be spread easily, about 30 minutes.

SAUSAGE, ONION, MUSHROOM & BISCUIT HASH

INGREDIENTS

> 8 oz sausages, breakfast or apple flavored

> Butter Drop Biscuits (page 21)

> 1 tbsp unsalted butter

> 1 tbsp corn or canola oil

> ½ medium yellow onion, chopped

> 8 oz (about 9 medium) fresh cremini mushrooms, brushed clean and sliced

> 1 sweet red pepper, seeded and coarsely chopped

> 2 tbsp chopped fresh flat-leaf parsley

> 1 tbsp chopped fresh oregano, or ¾ tsp dried oregano

> ¼ cup water or chicken broth

> Salt and freshly ground black pepper

> 6 large eggs, fried sunny-side up or easy over (optional)

YIELD
Makes 6 servings

Here is a new take on hash. The biscuits are broken into pieces, cooked in butter to brown them slightly, and then tossed with cooked sausages, onion, mushrooms, and seasonings. Top with a fried egg, if you like, and serve for Sunday breakfast, brunch, or supper. You can make corned beef hash by substituting the same amount of corned beef for the sausage.

METHOD Position a rack in the middle of the oven and preheat to 400°F.

Put the sausages in a pie pan, place in the oven, and bake until the sausages are browned, about 25 minutes, or less if the sausages are thin. Use tongs to turn the sausages for even browning. Transfer the sausages to paper towels to drain. Cut into 1-in-thick slices and set aside.

Break the biscuits into pieces measuring roughly about ¾ in. In a large frying pan, melt the butter over medium heat. Add the biscuits and any crumbs and cook, stirring often, until most of the edges of the biscuits are browned, about 8 minutes. Transfer to a bowl and set aside.

Return the pan to medium-low heat and add the oil. Add the onion and cook, stirring often, until it softens, about 4 minutes. Stir in the mushrooms and red pepper and cook, stirring, until they soften, about 5 minutes. Stir in the parsley and oregano and cook for 1 minute. Add the water or broth and deglaze the pan, stirring to scrape up the browned bits on the pan bottom. Stir in the reserved sausages and biscuit pieces and cook, stirring, until they are hot, about 3 minutes. Season to taste.

Divide the hash among warmed plates, top each serving with a fried egg (if using), and serve immediately. If you want to fry the eggs after you have finished preparing the hash, loosely cover the frying pan with aluminum foil and keep warm in an oven preheated to 275°F until the eggs are ready.

CHOICES Use a variety of fresh mushrooms in place of the cremini mushrooms.

RIBOLLITA

INGREDIENTS

> ¼ cup extra-virgin olive oil plus 2 tbsp

> 3 medium yellow onions, finely chopped

> 3 carrots, peeled and finely chopped

> 3 large celery stalks, finely chopped

> 1 cup lightly packed fresh
  basil leaves (about 24 leaves),
  torn into pieces

> 2 tsp finely chopped fresh sage
  (about 8 leaves)

> 2 tbsp finely chopped fresh
  flat-leaf parsley

> 2 large cloves garlic, peeled but
  left whole

> 5 cups beef or veal broth,
  low sodium if store-bought

> two 15-oz cans cannellini or other
  white beans, drained and rinsed

> 1 pound Swiss chard, endive,
  or savoy cabbage, coarsely chopped

> 2 tbsp tomato paste

> 1 bay leaf

> Salt and freshly ground black pepper

If you ever wanted to try a soup that is so thick you can stand a spoon in it, here is your chance. *Ribollita*, which means "reboiled," is a Tuscan soup that probably originated as a way of stretching leftover vegetable soup with bread to make another meal. The bread is layered with a white bean and vegetable soup and then baked.

METHOD In a large saucepan, heat the ¼ cup olive oil over medium-low heat. Add the onions, carrots, and celery and cook, stirring often, until softened, about 20 minutes. Add the basil, sage, parsley, and garlic and cook until the herbs are softened slightly, about 5 minutes. Add the broth, beans, chard, tomato paste, and bay leaf and stir well. Cover partially, adjust the heat to maintain a gentle simmer, and cook, stirring occasionally, until the vegetables are soft, about 1 hour.

Discard the bay leaf. Transfer 2 cups of the soup and the cooked garlic cloves to a food processor and process to a puree. Return the puree to the soup. Season with salt and pepper. (You can bake the soup with the bread at this point and serve it, or you can let the soup cool, then cover and refrigerate it overnight and bake it the next day).

Preheat the oven to 375°F. Arrange half of the bread slices in a layer in the bottom of a deep, 3-qt or larger baking dish. Ladle in half of the soup. Cover with the remaining bread slices and ladle in the remaining soup. Drizzle the remaining 2 tbsp olive oil evenly over the top. Bake, uncovered, until the soup is hot and the bread has soaked up the soup and thickened it, about 20 minutes if the soup is baked shortly after cooking or 35 minutes if it was refrigerated overnight.

Ladle into bowls, digging down to the bottom of the baking dish to ensure each diner gets both bread and soup, and serve at once. Pass the cheese at the table. Leftover soup can be reheated the next day and will be even thicker.

CHOICES You can cook dried beans for the soup for use in place of the canned beans. Sort 1 cup dried white beans, rinse well, and place in a saucepan. Add 1 yellow onion, halved; 1 bay leaf; and water to cover by 2 in. Bring just to a boil over high heat. Remove from the heat and let sit for 30 minutes. Return the pan to medium-high heat and bring to a gentle boil over medium-high heat. Cover, adjust the heat to maintain a gentle boil, and cook until the beans are tender, about 1¼ hours. Drain the beans and remove and discard the bay leaf and onion. The beans are ready to use, or let cool, cover, and refrigerate overnight before using.

> 8 thick slices An Everyday Crusty Round or Two (page 108), or 12 thick slices Crusty Artisanal Bread (page 49)

> Grated Parmesan cheese for serving

YIELD
Makes 8 servings

BLT CORN BREAD SALAD

INGREDIENTS

> 1 sweet red pepper, seeded and chopped

> ½ sweet onion, chopped

> 3 tomatoes, chopped

> 8 thick slices bacon (about 10 oz total), fried crisp, drained, and broken into bite-size pieces

> 2 tbsp chopped fresh chives

> 2 tbsp chopped flat-leaf parsley

> Freshly ground black pepper

> 1 cup mayonnaise, or more to taste

> Buttermilk Corn Bread (page 38)

> 1 cup pecans, toasted (see page 13) and coarsely chopped

> 1 head romaine lettuce, torn into bite-size pieces

YIELD
Makes 8 servings

Here is lunch, supper, or picnic fare in a bowl. Chunks of corn bread are tossed with vegetables, bacon, toasted pecans, and mayonnaise. Feel free to adjust any of the salad ingredients or quantities to your taste. Once the salad is tossed, it should sit in the refrigerator for no longer than 1 hour or it will get too soggy. You can, however, ready all of the ingredients 2 hours ahead and then toss them together just before serving. If you are transporting the salad to a picnic, be sure to keep it cold at all times and out of the sun. This is a good dish to make in the summer when garden-ripe tomatoes are abundant. If vegetarians will be at the table, leave out the bacon.

METHOD In a large bowl, combine the red pepper, onion, tomatoes, bacon, chives, parsley, and a few grinds of pepper and stir together gently with a large spoon. Add the 1 cup mayonnaise and lift and turn the ingredients to coat evenly. Break the corn bread into large, irregular pieces measuring about 1 in. You should have about 5 cups. Add to the bowl and mix gently with the other ingredients. The ingredients should not be heavily coated with mayonnaise. If you prefer a moister salad, stir in additional mayonnaise, 2 tbsp at a time. (At this point, the salad can be covered and refrigerated for up to 1 hour.) Sprinkle the pecans over the top.

Divide the romaine pieces evenly among 8 individual plates or salad bowls. Spoon the salad over the romaine, dividing it evenly, and serve.

WINTER PANZANELLA SALAD

INGREDIENTS

Tomatoes

> One 28-oz can whole tomatoes, drained

> 2 cloves garlic, sliced
  (14 to 16 slices total)

> 14 to 16 fresh basil leaves

> 2 tbsp olive oil

Salad

> ½ loaf An Everyday Crusty Round
  or Two (page 108) or Crusty Artisanal
  Bread (page 49), including crust,
  torn into bite-sized pieces

> 1 clove garlic, finely chopped

> 1 tbsp balsamic vinegar

> 1 tbsp fresh lemon juice

> 6 tbsp olive oil

> Kosher salt and freshly ground
  black pepper

Panzanella is traditionally a summer salad made with sun-ripened tomatoes and bread. This cool-weather version calls for roasting canned tomatoes with fresh basil and garlic, which brings out their sweet flavor. Bread for *panzanella* is often soaked in water, squeezed dry, and then tossed with the salad, forming crumbs. I prefer to toast torn pieces of bread and toss them in the dressing, so the bread absorbs the wonderful salad flavors but retains some of its crusty, chewy texture.

Piave cheese is a straw yellow, cow's milk Italian cheese with a sweet, slightly nutty flavor. It is carried in most cheese shops and in some well-stocked supermarkets. Look for roasted peppers in delicatessens or in the deli section of supermarkets.

METHOD Preheat the oven to 325°F. Line a rimmed baking sheet with two layers of parchment paper (the extra layer will prevent the tomatoes from baking onto the pan).

Prepare the tomatoes. Cut the tomatoes in half, and gently squeeze out and discard most or all of the seeds. Spread the tomatoes, cut-side up, in a single layer on the prepared baking sheet. You will have 14 to 16 halves. Put a garlic slice and a basil leaf on each tomato half, and sprinkle evenly with the olive oil. Bake until the tomatoes begin to color on their edges, about 1¼ hours. The liquid will blacken slightly on the paper liner as the tomatoes cook. Remove the pan from the oven and leave the oven on.

Discard the basil and garlic slices. Transfer the tomatoes to a bowl and set aside to cool slightly. (The tomatoes can be cooled completely, covered, and refrigerated for up to 2 days before continuing.)

continued ↘

WINTER
PANZANELLA SALAD

> 2 roasted sweet peppers, preferably
  yellow, cut into large bite-size pieces

> ½ cup lightly packed fresh basil leaves
  (about 12 leaves), torn into pieces

> 4 oz Piave or Parmesan cheese,
  cut into bite-size pieces

> 8 oz fresh mozzarella cheese,
  cut into bite-size pieces (optional)

> ⅓ cup pitted black olives,
  preferably oil cured

YIELD
Makes 6 servings

continued ↘

Make the salad. Spread the bread pieces on a baking sheet, place in the oven, and toast, stirring once, until lightly toasted, about 10 minutes. Remove from the oven and reserve.

In a medium bowl, whisk together the garlic, vinegar, and lemon juice until blended. Whisking constantly, add the oil in a slow, steady stream. Season with salt and pepper.

In a large bowl, combine the tomatoes, roasted peppers, basil, and bread. Pour the dressing over the top, then use a large spoon and large fork to toss and mix the ingredients together. Add the Piave and mozzarella (if using) cheeses and toss again. Sprinkle the olives over the top and let the salad sit for 15 to 20 minutes to allow the bread to absorb the dressing, then serve.

SALAMI, PROSCIUTTO, PROVOLONE & SWEET RED PEPPER STROMBOLI

INGREDIENTS

> *Focaccia dough (page 114)*

> *3 tbsp extra-virgin olive oil*

> *1 large clove garlic, finely chopped*

> *Freshly ground black pepper*

> *8 oz provolone cheese, thinly sliced*

> *4 oz salami, preferably Toscano, thinly sliced*

> *8 oz roasted sweet red peppers, cut into narrow strips*

> *4 oz baked ham, thinly sliced*

> *2 oz prosciutto, very thinly sliced*

> *½ tsp poppy seeds*

YIELD

Makes 10 to 12 slices

Stromboli sandwiches are long loaves filled with thinly sliced cured meats, cheeses, roasted peppers or other cooked vegetables, and sometimes fresh herbs. Bread dough is rolled out thinly, covered with the filling choices, rolled up jelly-roll style, and then baked. Delicatessens often sell slices of this delicious sandwich (for a hefty price), but making your own is simple and allows you to choose your favorite filling ingredients.

METHOD Make the dough as directed up to the point where you cover the bowl and let the dough rest for 10 minutes.

Position a rack in the middle of the oven and preheat to 425°F. Oil a baking sheet with olive oil.

On a lightly floured work surface, pat the dough into an 8-by-5-in rectangle. Cover with a clean kitchen towel and let rest for 10 minutes. This rest makes the dough easier to roll out.

In a small bowl, stir together 2 tbsp of the olive oil and the garlic. Set aside.

On a lightly floured surface, roll out the dough into an 18-by-10-in rectangle ¼ in thick. Position the rectangle with a long side facing you. Use a pastry brush to brush the garlic-oil mixture evenly over the dough. Then grind black pepper evenly over the dough. Leaving a ½-in border uncovered on all sides, spread half of the cheese evenly over the dough. Then spread the salami, red peppers, ham, and prosciutto evenly over the cheese. Spread the remaining cheese over the meats and peppers, and press gently to even the layering. Starting at the long edge nearest you, roll up the dough to form a tight roll. Pinch the edge and ends tightly to seal closed. The dough will stretch to about 19 in. Slide the roll, seam-side

continued ↘

SALAMI, PROSCIUTTO, PROVOLONE & SWEET RED PEPPER STROMBOLI

continued ↘

down, onto the prepared pan, placing it on the diagonal so it will fit. Brush the remaining 1 tbsp olive oil over the top of the roll, then sprinkle with the poppy seeds.

Bake until browned, about 35 minutes. Let cool on the pan on a wire rack for at least 15 minutes or up to 30 minutes. Using a large serrated knife and a sawing motion, cut into slices on the diagonal. Serve warm.

The roll can be tightly covered and refrigerated overnight. To serve, preheat the oven to 300°F and reheat the roll until hot, about 15 minutes.

CHOICES Fresh basil leaves or 1 tsp chopped fresh rosemary can be layered with the filling. Choose the deli meats you like, keeping the amount to 10 oz total. You can use up to 12 oz cheese. A medium-size onion, sliced and lightly cooked, can be layered with the other filling ingredients.

SLIDERS, MUFFALETTA & PANINI

Here are three popular sandwich-type preparations. The first, sliders, are typically small hamburgers and toppings on small buns. I have cooked the burgers and toasted the buns in a broiler, but you can also use a charcoal or gas grill.

Muffaletta is a New Orleans specialty. Salami, mortadella, baked ham, cheese, and olive salad are packed into a crusty bread loaf and baked. If you don't want to make your own olive salad, substitute 1/3 cup Karen's Food Company olive condiment (Karensfoodcompany.com).

Finally, panini, traditional Italian sandwiches, are usually made on crusty rolls or ciabatta and filled with a variety of meats and/or cheeses. They can be grilled or not. Here, I have layered Cheddar cheese between slices of cheese bread and slipped the sandwiches into a hot grill. Bits of cheese in the bread itself melt in the heat of the grill, resulting in the best grilled cheese sandwich imaginable.

YIELD
Makes 2 servings

INGREDIENTS

> *8 oz lean ground beef*
> *4 Sunday Lunch Dinner Rolls (page 89)*
> *1 cup sour cream*
> *2 tbsp prepared white horseradish*
> *4 tomato slices*

SLIDERS

Preheat a broiler. Divide the beef into 4 equal portions, and form each portion into a patty. Split the rolls in half horizontally.

Place the patties on the rack of a broiler pan and broil, turning once, until done to your liking. When you turn the patties, add the rolls to the pan, cut-side up, and toast lightly. (Or, you can toast them in a toaster oven.)

Meanwhile, in a small bowl, whisk together the sour cream and horseradish.

When the burgers and rolls are ready, liberally spread the cut sides of each roll with the sour cream mixture. Place a burger on the bottom of each roll, and top with a tomato slice. Close the rolls, divide between 2 plates, and serve at once.

MUFFALETTA

Preheat the oven to 350°F. Have ready a pie pan for baking the sandwich.

Make the olive salad. In a small bowl, stir together the olives, parsley, garlic, olive oil, and vinegar. Season with pepper.

Cut the bread round in half horizontally. Remove about half of the crumb from each half, and reserve for making bread crumbs. Spoon half of the olive salad, including the dressing, over the bottom half of the bread round and spread evenly. Spread half of the onion slices over the olive salad. Spread half of the cheese slices over the onion, and then stack all of the salami, mortadella, and ham over the cheese. Spread the remaining cheese slices and then the remaining onion slices over the meats. Spoon the remaining olive salad over the cut side of the top bread half. Replace the top half of the bread on the bottom half, and press gently to compact the filling ingredients. Place the filled bread in the pie pan.

Bake until the bread and filling are hot and the cheese has melted, about 15 minutes. Remove from the oven. Using a sharp knife, cut the large sandwich in half and divide between 2 plates. Serve at once.

YIELD
Makes 2 servings

INGREDIENTS

Olive Salad
> *3 tbsp pitted green olives, chopped*
> *2 tsp chopped fresh flat-leaf parsley*
> *1 tsp minced garlic*
> *3 tbsp extra-virgin olive oil*
> *1 tbsp red wine vinegar*
> *Freshly ground black pepper*

> *1 loaf An Everyday Crusty Round or Two (page 108)*
> *1 small yellow onion, thinly sliced*
> *4 oz provolone cheese, thinly sliced*
> *2 oz hard salami, thinly sliced*
> *2 oz mortadella, thinly sliced*
> *2 oz baked ham, thinly sliced*

GRILLED CHEESE PANINI

Preheat an electric panini grill or a griddle or frying pan and a panini press to medium. If there is a choice, use the ridged side of the press.

Spread one side of each bread slice with the butter. Turn 2 bread slices buttered-side down, and top them with the cheese slices, dividing them evenly. Top with the remaining 2 bread slices, buttered-side up.

Put the sandwiches in the panini grill or on the griddle and top with the press and cook until the bread is nicely browned and the cheese is melted and just beginning to drip down the sides of the sandwich, about 7 minutes. Using a wide spatula, transfer the panini to 2 plates and serve at once.

YIELD
Makes 2 servings

INGREDIENTS

> *4 slices Lots of Cheese Bread (page 111), each ¾ in thick*
> *1 tbsp unsalted butter, at room temperature*
> *4 oz sharp Cheddar cheese, sliced*

CHOCOLATE-GINGER BREAD PUDDING

INGREDIENTS

> ¾ cup unsalted butter, cut into pieces
> ¾ cup packed light brown sugar
> 3 cups whole milk
> 2 tsp pure vanilla extract
> 3 large egg yolks, lightly beaten
> ½ round loaf Sally Lunn Bread (page 112) or 1 Brioche loaf baked in a 4-cup loaf pan or brioche pan (page 56), preferably 1 to 2 days old
> 3 tbsp unsalted butter, melted
> 2 tbsp granulated sugar
> 12 oz semisweet chocolate, cut into ¼- to ½-in pieces
> ⅓ cup finely chopped crystallized ginger
> Powdered sugar for dusting
> Vanilla whipped cream (page 141), for serving

YIELD
Makes 12 servings

Sally Lunn Bread or Brioche is a perfect choice for making this bread pudding, which is flavored with rich dark chocolate and spicy crystallized ginger and baked in a large tube pan or soufflé dish. The crunchy topping is made from crumbs from the same bread used in the pudding.

METHOD Position a rack in the middle of the oven and preheat to 325°F. Butter the bottom, sides, and tube of a 9½- or 10-in tube pan with at least 3¾-in sides and a fixed bottom, or butter a 2½- to 3-qt round baking dish. Line the bottom with parchment paper and butter the paper.

In a medium saucepan, combine the butter, brown sugar, and milk over low heat and heat until the butter melts and the sugar dissolves. Pour the mixture into a large bowl, stir in the vanilla, and set aside for 5 minutes to cool slightly. Then whisk the egg yolks into the warm milk mixture. Set aside.

Cut the bread into ¾- to 1-in cubes. Put two handfuls of the bread cubes into a food processor and process to coarse crumbs. Transfer the crumbs to a medium bowl and stir in the melted butter and granulated sugar to moisten the crumbs. Set the crumbs aside.

Spread about one-third of the remaining bread cubes in an even layer in the bottom of the prepared pan. Sprinkle one-third each of the chocolate and ginger over the top. Repeat to make two additional layers of bread cubes, chocolate, and ginger. Pour the reserved custard evenly over the layers. The custard will not fill to the top of the layers. Sprinkle the prepared bread crumbs evenly over the top, filling any spaces between the cubes.

continued ↘

CHOCOLATE-GINGER BREAD PUDDING

continued ↘

Bake the pudding, uncovered, until the top is lightly browned and crusty, the custard is absorbed when you check the center of the pudding, and the pudding is set when you give the pan a slight jiggle, about 1 hour. If you are using a baking dish rather than a tube pan, the pudding may need to bake for an additional 10 minutes. Let the pudding cool in the pan or dish on a wire rack for 30 minutes. This allows the pudding to set up so that it can be unmolded. It will still be warm and the chocolate will still be soft when you serve it.

Use a sharp knife to loosen the pudding from the sides and center tube of the tube pan, or the sides of the baking dish. Invert a flat serving plate or platter on top of the pan or dish, and holding them firmly together with pot holders, invert them together. Carefully lift off the pan. Peel off the parchment. Invert a flat serving plate or platter over the bottom of the pudding, and holding the plates firmly together, invert the pudding again, so it is top-side up. Lift off the plate from the top.

Using a fine-mesh sieve, dust the pudding lightly with the powdered sugar. Use a large knife to cut slices, or a large spoon to scoop out portions. Top each serving with whipped cream and serve.

SAVORY & SWEET BUTTERS, SAUCES & SPREADS

Bread and butter is basic and a near-perfect combination, but these butters, sauces, and spreads can make good bread even better. Try serving lemon butter with Savory Lemon-Leek Loaf (page 25), blueberry sauce with Christmas Morning Belgian Waffles (page 34), and maple whipped cream with Pumpkin–Chocolate Chip Pancakes (page 33). Lemon curd is a thick, smooth buttery spread that is good slathered on almost any bread, but is especially nice on toast, popovers, or biscuits.

THYME OR THYME-GARLIC BUTTER

YIELD
Makes ½ cup

> *½ cup unsalted butter, at room temperature*
> *1 tbsp chopped fresh thyme*
> *1 large clove garlic, crushed (optional)*
> *⅛ tsp kosher salt*

In a medium bowl, and using a large spoon, stir together the butter, thyme, garlic (if using), and salt until well blended and smooth. Transfer to a small serving bowl and serve at room temperature. Or, cover and refrigerate for up to 1 week, then let stand at room temperature for about 20 minutes before serving.

To make herb bread, spread the butter on bread slices, wrap tightly in aluminum foil, and bake in a preheated 350°F oven until the butter melts and the bread is hot, about 15 minutes.

Other fresh herbs, such as basil, rosemary, or oregano, can be added to the butter or substituted for the thyme. Or, omit the herbs and use only the garlic to make garlic butter.

MAPLE OR HONEY BUTTER

YIELD
Makes ½ cup

> *½ cup unsalted butter, at room temperature*
> *¼ cup pure maple syrup or honey*
> *Pinch of salt*

In a medium bowl, and using a large spoon, stir together the butter, maple syrup or honey, and salt until well

continued ↘

continued ↘

blended and smooth. Transfer to a small serving bowl and serve at room temperature. Or, cover and refrigerate for up to 1 week, then let stand at room temperature for about 20 minutes before serving.

LEMON OR ORANGE BUTTER

YIELD
Makes ½ cup

> ½ cup unsalted butter, at room temperature
> 1 tsp finely grated lemon or orange zest
> Pinch of salt

In a medium bowl, and using a large spoon, stir together the butter, lemon or orange zest, and salt until well blended and smooth. Transfer to a small bowl and serve at room temperature. Or, cover and refrigerate for up to 1 week, then let stand at room temperature for about 20 minutes before serving.

CINNAMON OR SPICE BUTTER

YIELD
Makes ½ cup

> ½ cup unsalted butter, at room temperature
> 1 tsp ground cinnamon
> ¼ tsp ground nutmeg (optional)
> ⅛ tsp ground cloves (optional)

In a medium bowl, and using a large spoon, stir together the butter and cinnamon for cinnamon butter, or the butter, cinnamon, nutmeg, and cloves for spice butter, until well

blended and smooth. Transfer to a small bowl and serve at room temperature. Or, cover and refrigerate for up to 1 week, then let stand at room temperature for about 20 minutes before serving.

RUM, BRANDY, OR GRAND MARNIER BUTTER

YIELD
Makes ½ cup

> ½ cup unsalted butter, at room temperature
> 2 tbsp dark rum, brandy, or Grand Marnier
> Pinch of salt

In a medium bowl, and using a large spoon, stir together the butter; rum, brandy or Grand Marnier; and salt until well blended and smooth. Transfer to a small bowl and serve at room temperature. Or, cover and refrigerate for up to 1 week, then let stand at room temperature for about 20 minutes before serving.

CRANBERRY COMPOTE

YIELD
Makes 1½ cups

> 1 cup fresh or thawed, frozen cranberries
> ½ cup fresh orange juice
> 2 tbsp granulated sugar
> 2 slices fresh ginger, each ¼ in thick

In a medium saucepan, stir together the cranberries, orange juice, sugar, and ginger, cover and place over medium heat. Adjust the heat to maintain a gentle simmer and cook, stirring occasionally, until the cranberries are soft and some have split, about 15 minutes.

Serve the compote warm. Or, transfer to a bowl, let cool, cover, and refrigerate until chilled and serve cold. The compote can be refrigerated for up to 3 days.

BLUEBERRY SAUCE

YIELD

Makes 2 cups

> *3 cups blueberries*

> *2 tbsp granulated sugar*

> *1 cinnamon stick, 3 in long*

In a medium saucepan, combine the blueberries, sugar, and cinnamon stick over medium heat and bring to a gentle boil. Cook, stirring occasionally, until the blueberries soften but do not burst and the sugar dissolves, about 4 minutes.

Remove and discard the cinnamon stick. Serve the sauce warm. Or, transfer to a bowl, let cool, cover, and refrigerate for up to 3 days. Warm over low heat just before serving.

LEMON CURD

YIELD

Makes 1½ cups

> *6 tbsp unsalted butter, at room temperature, cut into pieces*

> *1 cup granulated sugar*

> *⅓ cup fresh lemon juice, strained*

> *2 large eggs*

> *2 large egg yolks*

> *1 tsp grated lemon zest*

In a heavy, nonreactive pan, stir together the butter, sugar, lemon juice, eggs, and egg yolks. Place over low heat and cook, stirring constantly with a wooden spoon, until the butter melts. Increase the heat to medium-low and continue to cook, stirring constantly, until the mixture thickens, about 6 minutes. To test the consistency, pull the spoon out of the mixture and draw your finger along the back; a trail should remain that does not disappear right away. Or, test with an instant-read thermometer; it should register 170°F. Do not let the mixture boil.

Strain the curd through a fine-mesh sieve into a bowl. Stir in the lemon zest. Press plastic wrap directly onto the surface and use a toothpick to poke a few holes in the plastic wrap to let steam escape. Refrigerate until cold, at least 5 hours or up to 3 days. If refrigerating for more than 5 hours, re-cover tightly with plastic wrap. The curd will thicken as it cools.

VANILLA OR MAPLE WHIPPED CREAM

YIELD

Makes 2 cups

> *1 cup heavy cream*

> *2 tbsp powdered sugar*

> *1 tsp pure vanilla extract*

> *2 tbsp pure maple syrup (optional)*

In a large bowl, using an electric mixer on medium-high speed, combine the cream, sugar, and vanilla for vanilla whipped cream, or the cream, sugar, vanilla, and maple syrup for maple whipped cream, and beat until soft peaks form. Use immediately, or cover and refrigerate for up to 1 hour.

INDEX ↗

TABLE OF↗↗ EQUIVALENTS

■ ■ ■ ■ ■ ■ ■ ■ ■ ■ ■ ◆

*The exact equivalents in the following
tables have been rounded for convenience.*

LIQUID/DRY MEASUREMENTS

U.S.	METRIC	U.S.	METRIC
¼ teaspoon	1.25 milliliters	½ cup	120 milliliters
½ teaspoon	2.5 milliliters	1 cup	240 milliliters
1 teaspoon	5 milliliters	1 pint (2 cups)	480 milliliters
1 tablespoon (3 teaspoons)	15 milliliters	1 quart (4 cups, 32 ounces)	960 milliliters
1 fluid ounce (2 tablespoons)	30 milliliters	1 gallon (4 quarts)	3.84 liters
¼ cup	60 milliliters	1 ounce (by weight)	28 grams
⅓ cup	80 milliliters	1 pound	448 grams
		2.2 pounds	1 kilogram

LENGTHS

U.S.	METRIC
⅛ inch	3 millimeters
¼ inch	6 millimeters
½ inch	12 millimeters
1 inch	2.5 centimeters

OVEN TEMPERATURE

FAHRENHEIT	CELSIUS	GAS
250	120	½
275	140	1
300	150	2
325	160	3
350	180	4
375	190	5
400	200	6
425	220	7
450	230	8
475	240	9
500	260	10